Ordinary People
and
UFOs

A Memoir of Contact

Lisey Clarkson

First published in Australia in 2024 by Lisey Clarkson

Email for correspondence: media@ordinarypeopleufos.com

© Lisey Clarkson 2024

The moral rights of the author have been asserted

All rights reserved.

Except as permitted under the *Australian Copyright Act 1968* (for example, a fair dealing for the purposes of study, research, criticism or review), no part of this publication may be reproduced, stored in a retrieval system, communicated or transmitted in any form or by any means without prior written permission.

All enquiries should be directed to the publisher.

ISBN 9780645858402 (paperback)
ISBN 9780645858419 (ebook)

 A catalogue record for this book is available from the National Library of Australia

Disclaimer

Ramtha®, C&E®, Consciousness & Energy®, Blue Body®, Fieldwork®, Neighborhood Walk®, The Grid®, Twilight® are trademarks and service marks of JZ Knight and JZK, Inc., a Washington corporation, and are used with permission. JZ Knight and JZK, Inc., do not necessarily endorse or support any of the views or commentaries, in part or in whole, expressed in this publication by its authors and editors.

For more information about Ramtha's teachings contact: Ramtha's School of Enlightenment, a division of JZK, Inc., P.O. Box 1210, Yelm, WA 98597, USA. www.ramtha.com

Cover image: Steve Alexander, Cherhill, UK, 2011

This book is dedicated to anyone who wants more than this world gives them

The most beautiful thing we can experience is the mysterious.
– Albert Einstein

Contents

Preface		vii
Chapter 1	The Eight Foot Indian	1
Chapter 2	The Implant	5
Chapter 3	The Gold Disk	11
Chapter 4	The Black Triangle	13
Chapter 5	The Diamond	20
Chapter 6	The Missing Hours	27
Chapter 7	The Boomerang	42
Chapter 8	The Owl	50
Chapter 9	The Green Rockets	58
Chapter 10	The Sonic Boom	65
Chapter 11	The Constellation	78
Chapter 12	The Shooting Star	84
Chapter 13	The Wobble	94
Chapter 14	The Mother Ship	102
Chapter 15	The Red Lights	108
Chapter 16	The Flash	115
Chapter 17	The Giant	122
Chapter 18	The Interaction	137
About the Author		151

Preface

The following manuscript recording my encounters with many different craft come with some responsibility. At times, they occurred with either or both of my two daughters, and I must consider the impact on their lives by publishing. My family too, and troublesome accounts recorded with people in my exploration of self aren't always flattering, but are relevant to what prompted the UFOs appearing, and need including. For these reasons I'm using a pet name given to me by my parents with my surname.

In this book, I explore difficult personal experiences because they demonstrate my motivations for doing mental disciplines that precipitated UFO visitations. More importantly, my dilemmas reiterate for readers that they can apply their own mental focus to overcome difficulties – and possibly have their own other-worldly encounters.

Whilst some craft were spontaneous visitations connected with retreats my daughters and I attended, the majority of them occurred during the application of disciplines that employ latent abilities in the brain. These techniques, learnt from a school of enlightenment, have interesting elements that readers may find unusual. Unapologetically, however, I have to say they work, and we had over a dozen of them as testimony. Real and tangible craft; some close enough we could have thrown a ball at them or touched them standing on our roof.

We learnt the practices from a being channelled through a woman in America's northwest. I understand that people would have an easier time accepting seeing UFOs before they can accept channelling a being nearly eight feet tall that lived 35,000 years ago, and who mastered this reality and ascended out of here. I get it. To me, now, I'm mature enough to know that this school is about learning to access the quantum field, and obviously this was of interest to off-world beings.

Here, I've attempted to explain what I did for UFOs to appear in a way that is easily understood; but I must include that the techniques don't belong to me, so I have only briefly outlined them in these pages. I've used trademarks where they are labelled, as is appropriate; and know that I have not been approached to endorse anything. This is my lovely story, and only my kids and a few close people knew they had occurred.

It must also be said why I settled quite deliberately on the title, which isn't flashy, I admit. At first, I wondered about using the modern term appropriated by UFO enthusiasts calling them UAP, but this didn't sit right with me, as this implies the vehicles cannot be conceptualised as very real objects. You will see, they were not nebulous apparitions, but were very particular shapes, colours, and materials. So, *UFOs* it was.

The *Ordinary People* aspect of the title was deliberately chosen because the techniques work for any person, regardless of one's past, class, education, spiritual persuasions, or lack thereof. No one is denied these opportunities if a brain occupies our head, as they have everything to do with science and our biology. Whilst I do associate these functions with spirituality – you don't have to subscribe to this to have results. That said, however, this book is a story of spiritual evolution, but without the dogma. I've intentionally included my fuckups and flaws, to example the notion that all parts of our life are purposeful, and there really is no judgment except our own. So, *Ordinary People* seemed suitably appropriate.

The appearance of craft described in here occurred infrequently, often with months or years between – and I was practicing disciplines a lot. This is to assure readers that if they seek to apply such disciplines, expect them to take time and extended input. Mine occurred over a period of about two decades, and from the end of 2016 to 2020 I was too destroyed in myself and did not focus at all – and naturally, no one came to visit. The good news is since applying them again I've had some lovely occurrences and visitors!

Why come out now after years of seeing the miraculous, and why a book and not YouTube videos, or relay my experiences to known UFO investigators? In short, I've been a high school teacher for decades, and I could never out myself in such an institution. Since I'm no longer a teacher, I now have an opportunity to share. This brings me to why I've chosen a book.

It's the disciplines that made these events happen. If I'd shared my story via regular UFO media, the deeper aspect of how these events occurred would be obscured by the sensationalising of the UFOs. I don't want this factor to be dismissed.

Here you'll find a lot of my own conclusions to things based on my experiences. If I'm referring to someone else's input, I'll credit them with their knowledge, and if my own wisdom has evolved out of others, you will know where and how I sourced them also. I don't purport to know everything, but I certainly illustrate what my fumblings have taught me and now know *how* to get where I'm going.

Lisey Clarkson

CHAPTER ONE

The Eight Foot Indian

A colleague, and friend, invited me to an event that strangely instigated the writing of this book. I'd been off work for some time, and as I was conscious of keeping up connections with people and friends, I agreed. She asked if I'd come along to a psychic night at a pub.

My first inclination was that it would be a rort. Surely the psychics would be full of shit, and I could even predict the type of clientele that would be attending the night. The fact that it was called *Bubbles and Spirits* immediately turned me off. My internal judgment questioned why psychics or spiritual mediums would sink so low as to garner participants using a night of drinking. A good business model, no doubt, but it narrowed down the target audience to a particular group of people I wasn't enthusiastic about. Either way, I was flattered she'd thought of me and made the effort.

The event hosted in the function room was packed with women. There's no need to explain why it was a hundred percent women, and anyone can equally surmise why they were there: love and money. At least I made my mind up that it was. I noted there were two groups of women, if I'm to generalise, which were roughly comprised of half over-dolled-up middle aged gals, and the other half equally polished young mums. The difference perhaps lay in the jewellery, with the older ladies probably wearing real gold, and the young ones wearing costume cheapies. My judgment of the group of over sixty women was pessimistic from the start.

Honestly, I was literally tolerating the event, wondering what the hell I'd said yes to. I watched as the two psychics did a group reading with the old, "I've got a grandmother coming through … she's telling me Michelle, Michaela? … anyone here this sounds familiar with?". Naturally there's going to be one or two, and you know how these things roll after that. This charade lasted for an hour, followed by food delivered while the psychics proceeded to give everyone a personal one-on-one reading.

My friend and I were at the back, and I could hear a lot of the subject matter given to those around me that were close enough to hear. It was the usual job, house, and relationship info that people had paid money to hear. And let's be honest – everyone is going to dismiss anything said that they don't want to know, me included. I actually couldn't wait to hear what garbage the psychic was going to give me, and I was ready to whip out my poker face when it was my time.

I had to make some entertainment out of this in my head, so I was prepared to not give anything away in my body language or tone of voice. Waiting to get my money's worth from my reading, and drinking the free drink received with my ticket, I decided I wasn't spending a penny more on this event that had already cost $75. When her time came for me, after hearing the usual dribble delivered to my friend that her guides were telling her she had some energy blocks, I was determined to make her work hard coming up with bullshit for me. I said nothing and maintained a dead-pan face and posture.

"You've got an Indian shaman standing behind you". 'Here we go', I thought, 'she's trying extra hard to impress me now', given my expressionless demeanour. "He's really tall … somewhere between seven and eight feet". My gaze on her intensified. Now she had my attention. None of us today have likely seen an Indian, or anyone for that matter, who was nearly eight feet tall. No one.

Chapter 1: The Eight Foot Indian

My BS radar began to retreat. If she was a fraud, then saying someone was that tall would be a gamble on her credibility, because ordinarily, hearing that particular detail would make any person laugh cynically inside and just enjoy the entertainment. Except: I'd been told these details about the entity who taught the disciplines at retreats I'd been attending. Hang in there if you're still sceptical like I was – it gets even better!

My friend, thankfully, was not the slightest bit interested in my reading, and was too busy texting all her other friends about what the psychic had said, which wasn't too interesting, as anyone could be given that generic feedback. On the other hand, mine was unfolding very differently than those I'd heard. As she proceeded, I glanced at my partner to double check she was adequately distracted to what the psychic then said.

"You've had UFOS around you all of your life". Let's pause here. A crowded room full of women with every reading being predictable, mundane responses, and suddenly I'm receiving UFO information? If she was making this up, then there would be a hundred percent chance I'd never seen one, so she was taking a risk for her reliability. What if I hadn't? And she said UFOs with a plural. Even if she had scoured the internet, she wouldn't have found this content about me; and there was no gain for her to say these things. In fact, she never asked my name to even suggest she had dug arduously around for a small seventy-five bucks to know my very protected secrets. My cynicism was immediately dispelled.

She said the Indian and aliens want you to write all your UFO experiences in a book. Okay, so let's assume she was a fraud, and making the whole lot up. To say one UFO may give her slight credibility, as anyone could think they may have seen one, but one incident does not make a book. Let's even give her the possibility of making up two UFOs – that's stretching the envelope – remembering too that she risked me saying I'd never seen any. But she didn't say one or two (two still does not equate a book), she stated, "visiting you all your life". She even said I'd been taken on board craft at times. Given the generalisability of her statements offered to all those around me, the topic of a nearly eight feet tall Indian and many UFOs was a stark and risky contrast to the others. These details, including her statements alluding to many, were spot on.

I'd occasionally wondered if I should write a book detailing these extraordinary things. I'm an English teacher, who's taught thousands of kids to write, and drafted several thousand essays, so why not?

Bloody hell.

CHAPTER TWO

The Implant

Only now, in deciding to write my experiences in mid-life, have I associated strange events from my past to the accounts you will soon read. I'd always wondered about them, but the incredibleness of seeing craft near me superseded them, and I simply forgot.

I've never felt any arrogance about these things happening to me, and never viewed them as validation that filled gaps in my self-esteem. In fact, I've never considered the real gravity of them until now, because I was always struggling to manage careless life choices. Additionally, I've recently concluded that I'm quite a slow learner – or a sucker for punishment – and if by chance there were selection criteria, in entertaining the idea that I may have been abducted or tracked by ETs, one would surely have to be for monitoring the effects of cortisol over extended periods of time!

Some UFO enthusiasts ascribe to the idea of a grand genesis project taking place on Earth – which is my theory too. However, with recent events occurring worldwide, I'm inclined to think, to some degree, that Earth has also been a prison planet. If these two possibilities were true, then this would explain why many of us may be tracked and observed, to understand Earth's human behaviours, genetics, and evolution. To the latter suggestion, of this planet being a prison, this would explain why evolution of people's minds is so forcefully stunted by religion, media, government, and medications, and adamantly keeping us focussed on war, sex, entertainment, and survival. Perhaps people resisting such concepts are worth watching from above. Irrespective of the 'why', for now, let's look at little events in my early life that foster a feeling of being monitored.

Going back to the '70s, when I was in primary school, there were a few times when I recall waking either sitting up at the end of my bed, or with my head held tightly down by firmly tucked blankets, laying back to front in bed. There's no doubt that many of us as kids have experienced this (can't say that I've talked about it to confirm), but oddly, and additionally, I often had my flannelette button up pyjama top on backwards. I vividly remember wondering how it was that I could have turned my head to where my feet should be, as in those days before feather doonas, we had heavy woollen blankets tucked in so hard you couldn't move. I can also recall the feeling of the collar pressed against my throat as I looked down wondering why the buttons were done up on my back.

At around eighteen or nineteen years of age, I had a little puzzling incident that I called my brother in to see. At the time, my family had moved to the Gold Coast after my dad retired from the air force, and my brother and I became close friends sharing the nightclub scene and surf culture.

As any teenage girl does, I was in front of the bathroom mirror wearing my togs to determine if my butt was any bigger than it was the day before. Curiously, I spotted a clear bubble of pink coloured plasma, or lymphatic fluid, atop a distinct hole just above the rear side of my right hip. The hole was only a millimetre in diameter, but visibly open down several more, with no graze or blood evident. I looked closer and was able to see down into the little hole, where I saw something black at the bottom of it. The thing was also visible

Chapter 2: The Implant

below the skin surrounding the hole, being an obvious triangular shape, about four millimetres wide on each side. I called my brother to come and have a look; and asking him if he could see what I was seeing, he agreed.

We were both puzzled; and had watched enough *In Search Of* and other UFO documentaries by then to wonder if it was an implant. At the time, I was quite excited at the idea of being taken up by aliens – I hadn't yet been indoctrinated about the terror of grey ones propagated by the media. Interestingly, I don't recall ever wondering about this event again until recently.

Before starting my university degree at around the same time, I found myself working in a health shop. Whilst the first year I regularly had Fridays off from trashing myself on dollar nights at my favourite club, I gradually became exposed to ideas about health, and wiping myself out naturally started to dissolve away. I'd also met a guy and was surprised to find his family were into health – and as readers can predict – they leaned towards spiritual ideas.

Retrospectively, I'm able to discern that my perception of spiritual topics decades ago was really lived like another religion. This also includes the way other people conducted themselves in spiritual matters in those days too. Everyone dressed the part, ate the part, and spoke the part. In all essence, the spiritual movement then was really another emotional experience. Feeling good about yourself and trying to feel good about others, but not really pushing any boundaries outside of what we'd been indoctrinated in our whole lives – living according to duality. Positive and negative, good and bad, things you must or mustn't do – and a crap load of guilt attached to the same things religions purported. Everyone – me included – were trying to be spiritual in a material world.

I'm still embarrassed when I recall some of the BS I floated around pretending to be, but that's all part of the experience; and I think I've now got the realism of science and practical application of the true meaning of spiritual, so I've just got to let it go. I'm still a bit uneasy using the word *spiritual* here, because there's so much attached to this term, and that also includes the word *God*. I would say, having applied mental disciplines and seen the incredible outcomes of them, that it's our interaction with the invisible field around us that denotes what *spiritual* means. And the elusive part of ourselves we use to engage with the field is what *God* means to me.

Consciousness, energy, and intent are the uncomplicated synonyms for these terms in my experience. It's religions that have put a bad taste in our mouths with them, and if they still make you uncomfortable, know that I get it. This book will serve only to demonstrate our interactions with the quantum field and the results we get from doing so. Good, bad, ugly – whatever we're doing is constantly interacting with the field, and if we can interact with it, then that makes us God, or Gods, if you will.

One of those look-back-and-cringe moments was a similar situation that I described instigating the writing of this book. I was around twenty years old, and in those days, I was on an emotional high belonging to a new group or philosophy, as the spiritual movement back then seemed to propagate. Dressed in all white flowing cheesecloth, among other people dressed in similar attire, and of course in a hexagonal building, the spiritual medium we'd come to hear addressed me.

She said I was being tracked by UFOs. Seriously, I was such a green horn back then that I had a gush of vanity for being singled out for some cosmic purpose. Let me also adamantly state, that on the drive home I couldn't ignore the silent onlooker in the back of my head, acknowledging what an inflated idiot I was: thinking I was somehow more special than the others there. I couldn't fool that all-seeing omnipotent parent – it knew when I was having myself on.

I now know that seeking to feel important, or neediness to be recognised, has nothing to do with confidence. It comes from rejection and denigration in childhood. The same for people who are perpetually nice, where their 'friendly meter' never varies. This has its roots in tempering a moody or volatile parent growing up, and I've observed both these tendencies in other adults who later revealed my suspicions. As I said: the spiritual movement back then only served to feel emotions, and everyone used it to fill voids in ourselves.

After completing a teaching degree, I allowed myself to fall pregnant, which in all honesty was my way of escaping the responsibilities of life – leaving home and working as an adult. I hadn't felt equipped to do these things, and in my impulsive imagination, I envisioned myself as a free-floating surfer's wife, with my kids growing up at the beach, as I'd seen some of my relatives do.

Without banging on about the emotional causes of this immaturity, I can isolate one cause behind my thinking: I wanted to be in control of my pathway, outside of what my dad wanted me to do. He wasn't wrong in his assumptions of me, when he said I was going to end up being a party girl with lowly retail or café jobs, and I had only gone to university to please him. I literally picked the easiest degree I could, with some modicum of interest in history as one of my teaching areas, and I literally partied and drank my way through the first half of it, barely passing.

Choosing to get pregnant at twenty-one was carelessly initiated, but that is a lesson I learned the hard way. I've come to realise, however, that it forced me to learn endurance. Unfortunately, however, this quality became a double-edged sword for the next three decades.

During the pregnancy, I was immersed in spiritual topics, reading books about reincarnation, and increasingly listening to channelled teachings about personal enlightenment. There were two notable and peculiar dreams I had during the pregnancy, that could possibly be attributed to the material I was engaging in, but I have since speculated they were more than that.

I recall having an afternoon nap one day where the dream had no content. And I mean no visual or audio content at all. I can only describe the dream as being a black void with no visible forms, and only the most intoxicating smell I recognised from my childhood of a particular perfume. I'd always envied friends whose mum owned the familiar brand cologne and wished desperately to have it. It was an extended dream of a singular experience – the consuming smell of violets. I remember when I woke up, I tried to go back to sleep for the all-encompassing smell, despite there being no form, light, or colour existing.

Similarly during this time, I dreamt I was being lowered in the dark through the air above my house. I could feel my long hair flailing upwards around my face as I was lowered effortlessly through the roof, where I woke up after floating down gently on the bed. I had heard years later, that abductions involve mind controlling people so they weren't frightened to possibly hurt the fragile little beings observing them. But, like the black triangle under my skin, I was too absorbed in life after my baby was born to consider these things thereafter.

Given that these were dreams, and people's imagination can inspire the weird content of them, they remain speculation for now. Such events, however, bear no comparison to material craft that uncloaked themselves for me in later years, where two different types appeared more than once to indicate some tracking may be occurring.

CHAPTER THREE

The Gold Disk

My first incident with a physical craft occurred a couple of years after, this time when I was awake and coherent. I never understood what it was at the time, and it wasn't until I was in my forties that I recalled this first sighting.

I'd been watching the X-Files television series at my mum's, a routine every Tuesday night I looked forward to as it was my night off from parenting. For a reason I don't recall, my daughter's father picked me up, and to get home we had to drive past the airport along a stretch of highway where the traffic was steady and roads well lit. Suddenly, a bright gold disk swished forward from above our heads, skimming over the cars in front. Despite being only a couple of seconds, I could see it didn't have lights as such, it was glowing gold over the entirety of the circular base, which appeared about two metres in diameter. I didn't see anything on the upper side of the disk, perhaps because this part was not illuminated, or because it was above me and so very quick. It appeared only as an incandescent disk.

I instantly thought we were about to be in a car crash, with the object that had 'fallen' from the sky landing on the cars in front. I grabbed the front dash with one hand and glanced at my partner to see if he was also bracing for impact. Instead, he and the cars ahead and behind us were all driving as if no one had seen the falling plane debris.

Contrasting against the quiet hum of the car, I excitedly asked if he'd seen it, and received only a subdued, "See what?". How could he not have seen it when it skimmed over the cars in front? Why did no one else slam on their brakes at the propelled object? It seemed as if he was driving trance-like, not unusual for a quiet drive home. Perhaps there was more to why he hadn't seen it.

It wasn't odd for me to suppose the falling object was a part of an aircraft, coming off and being flung down over a nearby highway. After all, we were next to the airport, and I'd experienced this once before in the mid '70s. Growing up as a child of an air force father, our family once lived on the fence line to the tarmac where an emergency landing took place.

I'd been in trouble in class and sent to sit outside the principal's office, which was highly preferable to classwork, and I played on the hand railing outside. Hanging happily in the morning sun, I soon noticed hordes of children and their teachers moving quickly out to the oval. I remember hearing what was going on from the admin staff, who were bustling around saying a piece of a plane was falling off – and the school was directly in its path. I became mildly concerned when I thought I'd been forgotten, when suddenly someone gestured for me to come with them. Arriving home that afternoon, it was terribly exciting to see all the news reporters and their cameramen in my backyard filming its sudden landing.

As such, the gold disk had no explanation in my imagination to make sense of, and I just assumed – somewhat confusingly – that the disk must've carved up the grass to the side in its crash landing, narrowly missing several cars and preventing a catastrophic pile up. Funny how I didn't wonder, moments after it sped over our car and others, where it may have dramatically landed and ricocheted flying pieces to. Like other events, I never thought about it after that until decades later when I saw it again.

CHAPTER FOUR

The Black Triangle

In my early years of entertaining spiritual schools of thought, I didn't consider that I had to engage in any physical or mental investment for my enlightenment. My understanding was limited simply to saturating myself with spiritual information. The emotional excitement of immersing myself in this genre filled the loneliness I was experiencing, after allowing myself to fall pregnant right before graduating from university.

I believed my fantasies growing up – and for years into adulthood. No surprise I only remembered the parts in fairytales where the handsome prince rescued the girl, never the meaningful parts like the fairy God-mother. I was always trying to force a future from my imagination, but all I ever got was a rotten version of it. I now know this habit was used to generate nice feelings when I couldn't escape my mum, who was always yelling and hitting me.

There was perpetual stress in our house, with her banging cupboards and bedroom doors, and a feeling someone was always doing something wrong. My dad's opposing reaction was to do more to please her, until by high school I can recall he did most of the washing, cooking, and preparing lunches for the next day. The more kindness he showed her the more disrespect he got, because on a primal level my mum preferred men with more grunt. And, pulled out of school by age eleven as an unpaid au pair for grandma's brood of babies, and her own at twenty, she'd already had a gutful.

When I was around eight years old, I began to scream back, mimicking what I was experiencing and perpetuating the days long torment in the house. A gentle man still in his twenties, my dad would always say, "Learn to bite your tongue and swallow your pride". I didn't know what pride was then, but both translated to tolerate abuse because aggressors were more important – and ultimately – that I was the cause of people's unhappiness.

Confusion thus became a theme that would permeate into my adult life. Having learnt that caregivers are simultaneously the source of protection and love with fear and derision eventually became a comfortable emulsion in my psyche. Deciphering what love is, or should be, has been a marked point of inquiry I've faced for decades.

While no doubt in society we blame the parents for lifelong emotional pain, because support and care go a long way, we could reduce our angst by understanding that living here is about perpetual learning over lifetimes. If we subscribe to reincarnation, the concept offers unlimited opportunities to figure ourselves out and accept that unfinished business purposefully generates the life ahead. It also gives credence to both nature and nurture, where our personality is comprised of incoming propensities that living conditions then elicit to the surface for realisation. I knew what I was entering into before I was born, and although I can't prove that, it's better than holding onto corrosive blame and hate all my life.

My mum and dad did a perfect job as actors on my stage, meticulously choreographed to spend most of my life seeking self-worth from others. Despite this, I will say from the outset that I love my parents, and they would become my greatest supporters in later decades. Everyone's backstory governs their interactions, and I am guilty of making my own mistakes that also affected my daughters.

If indeed our lives are by design, then who created them? If life has a precursive script, which is evident from the synchronicity of events nudging me in my life's direction, then this means the future is already known, and if so, somewhere in us already knows every outcome.

The confronting lack of friends, as everyone I knew was getting on and enjoying their new adult lives, and the realisation that babies can't be out at the beach all day, ripped apart the beach-bum-mum dream I'd had since childhood. My daughter's dad was also never home, because he didn't ask for this and we were wrongly paired, compounding the emptiness in my life.

I filled my own emptiness with spiritual teachings, largely audio tapes from Ramtha's School of Enlightenment. The teachings certainly did the trick of escaping into a world where I imagined anything was possible, but listening and recounting the teachings in conversation to my few friends left me exactly where I was: poor, depressed, and lonely. I could recite teachings like a thespian, but there was no material gain from information I'd absorbed. There is much to be discussed about the distinction between fantasising or holding concepts to materialise – one has emotion and the other doesn't. This is the key to using our mind to manifest, or running rampant on autopilot as I consequently did.

I remained working in health shops after my daughter was born, but decided to quit after realising teaching would be better paying. I also wouldn't have to smile and suck up to customers so they'd buy something, which felt so ingenuine. I was also sick of the shop owner's revelations with 'too much information' about his swinging spa parties, and the countless times when I dusted where he'd say he pictured me with fishnet stockings and a maid's suit. After I resigned, I sat outside the shopping centre wondering how the hell I was going to survive when I hadn't yet acquired a teaching job.

I was also ending the relationship with my daughter's father, and I was desperate to prove to my dad that I could rely on my own efforts to improve my life. Thus, while I awaited registration for teaching within the state system, I built up a little empire of private tutoring at nights. Unexpectedly, too, the education department had changed the registration criteria, and I had to complete another years' worth of university while I worked full-time.

There was no turning back at hearing this news, as I'd spent my last hundred dollars to register, and I'd quit my job on bad terms. My ex, who lived like Peter Pan skateboarding the streets and surfing most days, was himself unemployed, and my guilt in leaving him led me to pay for courses to better himself – and pay his maxed-up credit card. The latter started another habit of financially supporting men who couldn't get their act together. I suspect this was my way of garnering personal power, as I could feel sorry for myself and be a martyr at the same time.

I had to tackle starting high school teaching from scratch, undertake tertiary study on top of my tutoring, and raise my daughter on my own. This pivotal point marks where my pride to prove I wasn't a loser turned me into a self-sacrificing workaholic. In following chapters I outline how I worked harder not smarter, before realising too late this was going to destroy me.

I'd made a huge change to my circumstances, and with knowledge now, I opened myself up for the quantum vacuum to suck in a new reality. I recall exactly where I was when a spontaneous epiphany occurred regarding the spiritually spongy state I existed in. I was walking alone down a street near my house when suddenly I had an abstract knowingness: that enlightenment doesn't occur just because I listen and read things, but by doing the work to make it happen. I'd been saving my dollars to travel with my young daughter when this concept emerged, but this realisation was to offer a pivotal redirection to my life.

I was not proficient on the internet around the end of 1998, but I knew how to get on my dad's computer and search websites. Inspired by the concept of applying myself to enlightenment, I found the Ramtha school online and discovered serendipitously that they were beginning a world tour – with Australia on the cards in a few months' time.

I had a few thousand saved, which was huge for me. I'd earnt that money without relying on social services, as many single mums do in this country, and parting from it posed a serious setback to my bank account. I remember stewing over it. I recalled my ex-mother in-law telling me how she'd gone to Yelm, Washington, to do a retreat, and that Ram, as I fondly call him now, said to the audience if we truly understood his teachings we wouldn't need to keep attending his school. And she didn't. Thinking I must surely belong to those who 'got it', I'd never thought to go.

My curiosity to see Ramtha certainly egged me on, and I kidded myself that I'd kick ass because I was probably one of those select wise few who would march ahead, thinking I'd had ten years of teachings ahead of other attendees. With this youthful delusion, and my epiphany, I clicked on 'purchase' for myself and my daughter to attend in March 1999.

When you've been poor and scraping every penny, parting with it for the accommodation, attendance, and travel to and from, for one week, was terrifying. Suddenly I had nothing, and I seriously wondered if I'd done the right thing – which was too late then – it was done. And then the extraordinary happened.

My little one, then six, was sitting at our bedroom window, which wasn't screened for insects at the time, where we could rest on the windowsill and gaze out. We lived only about fifty metres back from the highway, and being central to shops and cafes, the neighbourhood was aglow with streetlights and cars. "Mum!", she called, "Come and see this, quickly!". Running from the next room, it didn't take a second to know that the black triangle slowly emerging from above our heads, was not of this world.

When something like this occurs, I can adamantly say: there is no fear. Absolutely none. In those moments, it is so beyond anything one could experience that it elicits only awe and wonder. It truly exists outside of any predictable experience we could reference it to – and we literally have no emotion attached to it.

We were both silent and watching. Ever so slowly, and in my opinion deliberately, it floated over us into full view. In my mind I heard myself say 'stare at its parts to take it all in, so you can remember it'. I made every effort to look at it all, and it gave me the time to do so. Being dinner time, the suburban lighting provided unhindered vision for us to sufficiently absorb every detail. Its proximity to us was such that if we were on our roof, we could have brushed our hands along its base as it gently passed above.

It was completely black, smooth, and shiny in texture. At about three or four metres wide, it travelled with one point forward and the other two points to the rear. Underneath I could see shapes and parts, and on each corner, there were black balls of the same colour and material, about a foot and a half in diameter. As it emerged in full view between our house and the neighbour's, it was evident there were no windows. Focusing intently, I saw on each of the three sides of the base that there were moving pieces, sliding back and forth in unison along the edges. Completely silent, with no light emitted, it moved with a gentle horizontal glide.

I wondered then, and still do, about the occupants. The height of the craft was no more than a metre, and if there were pilots, they must've been tiny! In following years, after seeing quite a few with limited space, I often wondered about the being's sizes. Since the variety of spaceships were completely different in their appearance, I presumed they must be different races. After interactions with them, I pondered over the years if they knew me somehow, or if it was simply the affect my focus, or my brain, was having on the quantum field around us to attract them. Over the years my thoughts on this have evolved, as I evidence throughout the book.

In this first monumental encounter, I knew immediately that this visitation was associated with my retreat. I just knew it. It was confirmation for something I'd ummed and ahhed about engaging in, and it exceeded any expectation one could have imagined in response to my doubts. I hadn't deliberately asked for any sign if what I'd paid for was right, as I didn't think like that then. I'd accepted from Ram's teachings that we make our own reality, not wait for it by some luck or chance. This was too far out – unimaginable – and occurred concurrently with my worry. Yesssss! I was on to something very big.

CHAPTER FIVE

The Diamond

After this experience I was propelled into the new future, and it was difficult keeping my excitement to myself. Being the nineties, and working in a high school, there really was no scope to share this with staff I'd befriended – and certainly not with impressionable teenagers. By attending events thereafter, I began to harbour a sense of having to hide things for the next two decades, as if it might metaphorically have led me to being burnt at the stake. I'm not exaggerating. The fear of being found out for having spiritual beliefs – and having UFOs appear – felt like keeping a life-threatening secret. Back then, it wasn't everyday language to talk about our minds affecting the quantum field like it is somewhat now.

Before returning to my first retreat experience, let me add that a student in one of my classes also saw the same craft. Months after our experience, a boy in one of my medieval lessons on witchcraft, which often invites conversation out of the box when you teach such topics, piped up that he'd seen a UFO. When I asked in front of the class what he'd seen, he said, "a black triangle, one night at Palm Beach when I was riding my pushy" – exactly the same encounter, and also where it had occurred for my daughter and me. Without anyone seeing, I later whispered that I'd seen this one too.

Chapter 5: The Diamond

Attending my first event, I arrived sick as a dog. My daughter and I had overnight trained it down to Sydney from Queensland, in warm climate clothing and Antarctic air-conditioning. I'd had no sleep from sitting up all night and freezing my ass off to boot! If I thought I was going to be an adept and absolutely smash these disciplines, I was in for a rude awakening.

The disciplines were not as I expected: no sitting still meditating to nature sounds, or simple deep breathing, and no basking in my imagined auric glow. They were designed to get us out of laziness, and all the usual distractions of hunger, being noticed by others, or needing to have an afternoon nap after a morning of easy listening. Instead, Ram had us blind-fold on a field all day, focussing on cards in the relentless sun; bumping into fences, lady's fingernails, and impatient people slamming you – emphasising that you impeded their way with their exaggerated shoves.

The hidden cards contain a desire coloured in symbols or words by participants, and there can be hundreds on the fence across several rungs. There is no way you can find yours by chance; trust me, I've since done untold number of hours to know. It was everything representative of chaos and frustration we could possibly experience to remind us of our spoilt, whinging self. The mastery lay in moving past this emotional weakling, and in brief moments when you could, you'd be sublimely drawn to your dream-sketched card by surrendering to your deeper mind. Unfortunately, this seemed to be occurring for everyone else but me.

During this week, it seemed impossible for me to find my drawn dream, and I became very disappointed in myself. On the last day of retreat, I was so fed up that I said in my head, 'Come on focus; you've paid so much money to be here, don't waste it!'. With what limited effort I could draw; I went hard within myself – in my mind. Suddenly something weird started to happen.

Like one of those huge magnets we see in cartoons, my body started being pulled to the right. I was literally stumbling side-ways in a fast-paced jig as it dragged me, but I went with it. As usually occurs when we're really focussed, no one was in my way, and I eventually hit the fence. With genuine trepidation I opened the sealed card. Blow me down, it was mine! I had my first real win in applying the disciplines. I was absolutely aglow with my personal triumph, and I'd done it all by myself. The pulling I'd felt was not a slow crab walk sideways, but other-worldly, full-body pulling, which gave a brand-new edge to my understanding of the connection of the body to the spirit. It was now real, and not just words I used to read and hoped were true.

Over the years, I used to wonder why Ramtha didn't just manifest for us when we struggled, to prove the teachings were true. Now decades on I realise it isn't about him. It's about us. How on earth could it sink in that we were divine, and had access to magic by using our brains for everything if we weren't forced to access it? It was more than simple. And it has taken me too long to understand that focus is easier than working myself to the bone to have something.

After this experience, I went home with solid confirmation that my ordinary brain, with all my baggage, could source myself to make things happen. This is not to say I was changed. No way. It has been an ongoing process the last few decades, with shitloads of adversity to wake me the fuck up. Despite my small supernatural event, I remained stubborn to my old ways, killing myself inside as I went.

My little accomplishment of not giving up was obviously observed by others who must've found it worthy of rewarding me. The Sunday evening, after returning home in the afternoon, was followed with my usual ritual of strolling down to another single mum who had two daughters to catch-up. I wanted to share everything, such as my triumph on the last day and incredible information learnt on esoteric topics, but I knew my friend well enough to know that she really wasn't interested in these things, and it wasn't the nature of our friendship anyway. As such, I shut up and let the couple of hours progress as they always did, with ordinary chit chat. At around

Chapter 5: The Diamond

6:00pm I gave my farewells and walked ahead of my little girl to our friend's front yard.

At this time of the evening, just after sunset on the Gold Coast, the highway that runs parallel to the beachfront from top to bottom of the city is reasonably busy. It's a major double-laned road linking many suburbs in a narrow strip; and on Sunday nights there's a lot of movement as people leave the coast to return to Brisbane or pass over the nearby border to New South Wales. The beaches are also popular with locals, who frequent them with their families for whatever leisure, and many are returning from a day out. My friend's house was about 40–50 metres back from the highway, and a small shopping centre with a supermarket was in the next street facing the highway. Thus, I could hear steady traffic all around me, and car and street lighting added an emanating golden glow to the neighbourhood.

As I think every human being does when waiting outside, I immediately looked up at the night sky. Directly in my vision, at about 45 degrees, and approximately 50 metres above the next street was an absolute wonder. There, in its lit-up brilliance, was a huge diamond craft. The object was silver metal in material, with two rows of very bright white lights: one row around the widest perimeter, and another smaller one running parallel along inside of that. I could see the bottom protruded somewhat below, in another smaller diamond shape where the inner light perimeter followed, so it was not completely flat underneath as the black triangle was. No mechanisms or shapes were on the belly of it, just plain silver illuminated by two rows of white lights. Because of its position above me, I could only see the underside, and therefore no windows were visible. It was completely still and silent, and no operating systems, engine parts or exhaust were evident to keep it static and elevated.

I was spellbound.

I have to say that somehow I knew it was there for me. It was there in all its brilliance with no one else present. Given that it coincided with my return from the retreat, I knew it was some kind of reward for me taking a risk in giving up my savings, to learn how to use my own brain and apply it in my small capacity. No one was going to believe me, so I could only keep these beautiful secrets to myself and my little girl. There is nothing gained for the arrogant personality if we can't share it to anyone, but it was huge confirmation for taking steps to self-mastery.

Surprisingly, I had the wherewithal to think in those few moments to communicate with it, or rather, its occupants. I didn't understand then how advanced extra-terrestrials may be connected in consciousness to all that is, but I did accept that their technology may be advanced enough to read my mind. In my head, I said spontaneously to the people on board, 'If you love the God that is in me and you, then you're allowed to take me up'. That may seem the strangest thing to say in these unimaginable few moments, but there was no preconceived line I had rehearsed in case it happened – it just came into my head. Readers may be distracted by my use of the term 'God' being 'within' people, and this deserves further explanation.

Firstly, I am compelled to say that I have never subscribed to any religion. The monotheistic religions, meaning having one singular god of Judaism, Christianity, and Islam, have taken God out of the people and nature and placed it as an old man somewhere above us. Let's not forget: a judgmental and persecutory one at that. This has never resonated as truth to me, and I suspect if you're reading this book, you may also be on the same page in this regard. But, for those still on the fence, I'll quickly add the historical concepts of God that I subscribe to.

If we explore any gnostic or pagan material, we'll discover that ancient people used to accept God as the essence in everything that allowed it to exist. In fact, very ancient pictographs and texts display this essence as being feminine, if we are to think in human terms of gender. This ancient understanding seems logical given females give birth, so people originally saw all creation with this principle. Take

Chapter 5: The Diamond

a look online and you'll find there exists thousands of prehistoric handheld objects with full breasts and tummies, known as Venus figurines; or search Egyptian tomb paintings of the naked goddess Nut laying over all life below her. That said, however, I prefer to think of God as consciousness, and not in terms of gender at all. Thus, this was my preface for including the statement to the diamond wonder, and my consent to be taken onboard was given in this context.

I had heard by then via UFO documentaries, largely concerning abductions, that aliens could be frightening and invasive, such as greys, or even reptilians, who were reputed to be cruel and controlling of humans. Thus, in a sense, I was differentiating between the groups of ETs, as I was crudely aware of them, to give permission to those who were kind and guardian-like.

Again, my concepts and conclusions of ETs then was so limited. I doubt very much that a malevolent race would've bothered to present itself in open glory for me to observe after attending a spiritual retreat. After all, in my eyes I was just a nobody in the scale of all things, so I knew there was something just and kind for that display. My understanding of the different races has evolved over the years, and I no longer am afraid of the 'baddies' as I was before.

Interestingly, like the first gold disk I'd seen some years before, I had a moment during this encounter that resembled my first occasion. I wondered if cars travelling to-and-fro were about to have a huge crash as their eyes caught sight of the brilliantly lit vehicle. Surely the numerous drivers, literally driving towards it from each direction of the highway, and those walking out of the shopping centre below on the next street, could see it? A peculiar thought to have in those precious moments, but it was so huge, low, and spectacularly lit up that everyone driving past in that moment must've seen it. As I wondered these things, I again heard only the steady flow of passing cars just metres up the street, humming by undisturbed and undistracted.

When I'd had a few seconds to view this diamond wonder, and communicate remotely to it, I was left with the question: who are the occupants? Were they an assembly of mixed races? Were they human-like, or varying types of grey beings? A craft alone seems devoid of any occupants because that's all we see in those instances, but when we realise beings must be in there controlling its movement, that's mind bending.

It wasn't until years later that I began to spend considerable time wondering if they knew me, which I never contemplated at the time. There was no one else on the street to view it, and this materialisation of a second one at the conclusion of my attendance at a school of enlightenment led me to see this uncloaking as personal, in a kinship kind of way. If I'm an ordinary human on a crowded planet, how did they know what I was engaged in to warrant a visit? And how did they know exactly where to find me in that moment? This sort of questioning leads to conclusions that they must have mastery over time and space, beyond what our simple minds can imagine. Such good contemplations.

The moment I gave permission to take me up, the diamond's lights increased their intensity on every side, including the lower row. A second after this, it accelerated sideways so fast, that it caused a blazing trail of white light, before vanishing in moments before my eyes.

Two close and physically manifest craft on either side of my initiation into the arcane: they had to be related. I'd had my confirmation.

CHAPTER SIX

The Missing Hours

When the original fantasy of the life I wanted didn't work out, a new one aptly surfaced. Again, deaf to reality that this was probably not a good move, I set about enforcing the new one. At that stage, I believed the feelings imagery generated were the source of manifesting; but looking back, it's obvious I was just lolling about in lala land to mask my lack of – well – everything.

I could accept by then that life was changeable using my mind, but I was mistaken in thinking how this process worked. I now know that when we force into being our imaginings, we aren't creating anything at all. The fantasy is in fact our soul pulling us into a drama we were already meant to have. The original program – a life by design. In my case: it was an extremely patient one, as I've taken the hardest path every bloody time.

Before moving on, a tidbit on how I later determined why we don't *feel* anything in order to manifest a new reality: feeling always comes after the event. For example, imagine yourself doing something exciting. Note how a feeling comes *from* this. It's the same as watching a movie, where we see a riveting scene then feel it in our body a moment later. If feeling comes *after*, then it's the product of experience, not the precursor.

Similarly, when we go over and over in our head about a fantasy that feels so delicious, we're living it in our head. The brain doesn't know the difference between real or imagined, as we proved with the movie example above; and anyway, the intent of the soul is to deliver the experience as it was already planned – not as we desire. For me, it was to understand where self-worth comes from – or doesn't come from, more accurately.

I continued attending Ramtha's school off and on from '99, as once you've experienced magic, you become absorbed and want to know more. I wouldn't say I had any notable gains, or real demonstration of the knowledge I absorbed, because of my fierce loyalty to my emotions and the pretences attached to them. This understanding has taken until now to come to terms with. Mastery over the body and brain is a lifelong process, and possibly many lifetimes more. Instead, I continued to rely on other people's minds to acquire spiritual knowledge: sucking in content from books, CDs and the internet when it came about, but I never quite understood the application of disciplines for actualising my own growth.

I'd read so many incredible esoteric books before and during this early period in Ramtha's school, but there were a couple I was utterly compelled to read. I saw the titles, knew little to nothing about them, and though they appeared rather ordinary on the covers, I had to have them. Compared to others – these were totally captivating. I'll step into the first one by introducing a direction my life took that led to me living in Egypt in 2003. This experience eventually ties into the first extraordinary book I had to have.

Back then, I had a mix of international flatmates, who collectively consolidated a new fantasy I'd been brewing for a couple of years since ending the relationship with my daughter's dad. This one had the new and exciting twist of being a free-spirited wanderer, traveling with my young daughter to mysterious places, with equally

Chapter 6: The Missing Hours

exciting rendezvous. As my original program would have it, ever nudging me gently into my next drama, I'd watched Kate Winslet's film *Hideous, Kinky* about this exact idea, where my next instalment was discreetly ignited. Building on this metaphor, of a slow burn, it was to become my own trial by fire.

My flatmate's imprints were soulfully orchestrated, as I've come to learn. I had a bombshell, beautiful girl from Turkey, who abhorred the Muslim upbringing she'd had; a gorgeous, irreligious Italian man from Rome; and two Israeli guys, who also recoiled from their Jewish society, faking military service documents to avoid holding guns towards innocent Palestinians. Their irreligious stances lulled me into confidence that the ancient countries of the Mediterranean were more cosmopolitan than 60 Minutes had led me to believe. I booked tickets to travel from Egypt through to Turkey, and in the interim I met a man online in Cairo who looked remarkably like my Italian friend. Because of this likeness, and the blind assumption I had that these cultures must be more modern than I expected, I fell naively into my new reality.

You can probably predict the outcome. Lonely, exhausted single mum meets third-world, middle eastern man with a good enough command of English to suck a westerner in. Again, I was stubborn to my dream, and when my new man said we should marry so no one could break us up, it felt right out of a movie, and I didn't hesitate to oblige.

In the Justice department, when we were waiting to be married, I heard very loudly in my head, 'You're making a big mistake'. I couldn't ignore it, and knew it came from that part of me that silently watched everything from the back of my head. Trying to decide if I should back out, I went to the toilet. The bowl was filled to the top of the enamel with fermenting, slushy sewerage. I even wondered if my own contribution would cause it to overflow onto my feet. What a befitting representation of what lay ahead.

Whilst there, I noticed two other Aussie women waiting to marry middle eastern men. I saw that both ladies were obviously older, and for all intents and purposes, they were ordinary looking women. The youthful, olive skin of the Arabs contrasted with the weathered skin us Aussies of Celtic descent are prone to here. I wondered why they couldn't see the guys were in it for their ticket out of poverty.

The day we married, he gave me the "If you love me, you'll be a muslim" speech. He tried his best to sell Mohamed's life and described how he'd been taken by God on a sheep through the air to Jerusalem. "Did you say ship or sheep?", I asked, given his accent. I'd be slightly more inclined to believe ship over sheep, picturing a UFO of course. He repeated himself twice that it was a sheep, "as in baaaa", after which I stormed off. The next morning when he went to work, he locked the deadlock on the apartment door. This should have rung alarm bells.

In the meantime, my dad, who'd been a passive man all my childhood, was desperately worried enough to try to stop me coming back for my daughter. When I came home from this first visit to Cairo, he'd taken her passport. I went to three police stations to appeal to them to have it returned with little interest. Imagine explaining to the police officer that you'd met a guy online, in an Islamic country a year after the 9/11 event, in the early days of the internet. The cop at the third station, however, jumped on the phone and told him that unless he'd had a court order saying so, he had stolen my personal property.

To those around me, entrenched with the notion of terrorists infiltrating Western nations, it looked like my mental capacity had been hijacked and my own plane was set to kamikaze – and god knows what else. Disregarding the genuine fear held by my loved ones at the time, I was swept off my feet by emotions and was incapable of being stopped by any intervening logic. If I could ignore the loud warning from my spirit while waiting to be married, I certainly wasn't going to listen to my own flesh and blood.

Whilst I wasn't cognisant of it for years, it's ironic that the film initiating my dream as a nomadic mum was set in an Islamic country with a handsome muslim playing the saviour. When I had my messenger chat set up with the help of my Turkish friend for communicating with her and our international friends, it did not comprise of seeking love on the internet. I had little understanding of this then, and in the months I used it, I only received one request to chat in a world of infinite users, and that was with my future husband. I had already bought my ticket to Egypt before this, and the peculiar coincidence of having a singular request from one man close to my age in Cairo now seems very purposeful to the tibulation that later unfolded. Like a pinball nudged gently in directions seemingly random, I know that this journey was meticulously predesigned for me to discover the real source of worth and love.

Having my daughter's passport returned didn't pose any significant relief, however, as my parents had taken her out of her primary school in my absence and enrolled her in another, with themselves as the guardians. When I went to the new school to collect her, the principal asked me to leave the grounds like an abductor since I was not registered as her parent on the enrolment. My daughter's eyes, as I was told to immediately leave, were harrowing, and my shame was indescribable.

I found out shortly after that my dad had told her she most likely would never see her mum again, and to this day she says she has pain regarding this. To impede me further, my dad served court papers to have her removed from me for choosing to take her to Egypt. I was devastated to read that he'd said things that were utterly untrue; naturally he wanted his case to be solid, so he was going to pull out all punches to protect his granddaughter from whatever he believed the media had persuaded him to think.

I stood my ground with childish conviction until he relented, wherein I immediately packed our belongings and took her to live on the Nile. On arriving, I couldn't hide from the inner voice that perpetuated for days, and into weeks and months, 'What have I done?'. I had no school organised, had no money – and neither did my husband. I chose to ignore it; my pride had in no way subsided, nor was it for years to follow.

During this agonisingly boring year in Egypt, we had one minimal reprieve when we holidayed at Alexandria for a few days, with my husband's family friends. On one occasion there, I was politely berated for hours about being a muslim for my husband. I sat with a woman wearing a hijab and, allegedly, the third highest judge in Egypt. When we arrived, there were little brown balls of hashish lined up along the balcony railing, where the pair took turns burning them down a shisha pipe for the night. I interrupted the judge at one point and asked if he'd sent people to jail for using drugs. He didn't hesitate at all to say he did, and I informed him that I thought I was more moral having no religion than he was having his.

Despite my own personal ignorance, I was observant of the intriguing juxtaposition of the ancient and modern cultures of Egypt. Cairo spills out so expansively, that the pyramids are on the doorstep of a concrete jungle. We will always see a backdrop of desert on TV, but if the cameras faced the other three sides, we'd see they're on the fringe of a giant city. On a public bus once, I saw the pyramids between high rises, and it struck me how Cairo's present architecture seemed so crude compared to the prowess of the ancient builders.

Similarly, the religiosity and backwardness I'd observed in the people I was mixing with was really surprising. I only associated with the upper middle class and educated Egyptians, who I anticipated would be more worldly and critically thinking. I had an inkling that perhaps religion had been its original downfall. After this factor, I surmised that being introduced to high society under the French, and then the British, the latter of which withdrew in the middle of last century, left them stuck between worlds. Everyone we associated with lived off inheritances from wealth garnered under the former British Empire with no dedicated thought about its sustainable use or making it into more.

Chapter 6: The Missing Hours

After seeing the ancient monuments myself, and having taught the subject for decades, I have concluded that the majority of academic interpretations of ancient Egyptian civilisation may not be as enlightened either. I cannot extract any plausibility of an ancient race managing to build colossal structures, sculptures, and tombs, into the single finite idea proposed by historians and anthropologists, that their architectural efforts centred around an afterlife. That's saying on the one hand they were geniuses of engineering, but on the other, simpletons who believed they'd need their trinkets on the other side.

I mean, do they really think Kings and Queens commissioning feats of wonder would be so trivial as to believe they'd need their underwear, chairs, beds, and jewellery in a non-physical afterlife? Tutankhamen had nearly 150 loin cloths in his! It seems that humans are only able to conceptualise as big as their present experience; and given the influences of religion in our literary and cultural history, there is generally a default to make decisions cloistered by our own beliefs of veneration and burial practices.

Even more ridiculous is the conclusion drawn by academics that the pyramids were built as tombs. This assumption, and it is a weak assumption if one is to rely on judgments based on evidence, just doesn't cut the cake for me. The greatest tombs found in both valleys of the dead are elaborately decorated warrens of underground rooms and tunnels, covered in detailed paintings depicting their entire lives. In striking contrast, the pyramids at Giza are absent of any inscription concerning their lives, much less even their name! See the contradictions in logic and common sense here? No coincidence then, that they're termed the wonders of the world – no one can be truly satisfied with these answers.

If you desire to know other theories, take a look at *The Nine Faces of Christ* by Eugene Whitworth and *Initiation* by Elizabeth Haich. These may not provide factual descriptions of the pyramids using evidence, but they certainly provide plausible purposes for their construction worth pondering. I am not surprised that a friend lent me the latter author's book, coincidentally while I was in Egypt. Haich's explanation of the purpose for the pyramid shape literally blew my mind. When I included it for practising hypothesising in my history lessons students would all simultaneously have their mouths open, staring at the profoundness of the design and its meaning. I even had one polite footy boy respond with, "Fuuuuuck!", and all I could say was, "I know!".

As I learnt more information over the decades about ancient knowledge, spiritualism and enlightenment, my lessons around religion in history also evolved. I could captivate young people with integrated concepts and critical thinking to allow them to form their own conclusions, instead of telling them what the 'truth' was. I didn't need to indoctrinate them – when the cacophony of ancient symbolism is paired, it's undeniable.

One does not even have to subscribe to esoteric ideas when marvelling at the absolute size and feat of the pyramids built millennia ago. I'm sure many people wonder, across a wide spectrum of possibility, if we've either lost something intellectually since then, or that aliens built them. They're on sand for god's sake, and no crane on this earth could assemble these gargantuan structures.

Cairo offered very little to do from a westerner's perspective. The museum therefore posed a decent time filler for my young daughter and I; and in there we didn't have cars with young men constantly swerving over to the side of the road asking if we wanted to be 'friends'.

Since I'd married a local, the museum price was reduced to 25c each in Australian currency – a perfect escape since we were skint. Naturally most people are familiar with King Tut, the boy king, as well as other figures such as Ramses the Great, Nefertiti, and Cleopatra, the last pharaoh in its history. Interestingly, I'd never come across Akhenaton, King Tut's father. Odd really, having learnt

Chapter 6: The Missing Hours

about Tutankhamen in school and taught it myself, I'd never heard of him.

Within the museum, there are several floors, and an endless assortment of painted sarcophagi, wall reliefs, statues, and papyri, showing one art style across thousands of years. They used what is termed *frontalism*, and there's no deviation across the timeline of ancient Egypt – except for one enigmatic man. Frontalism is where the characters are always depicted with their hips and legs facing sideways, the chest facing the viewer, and the head in profile. The characters usually have the pharaoh drawn much larger in scale than their wives and children to show their rank above the others, too. Similarly, statues have the very linear, rigid forms, all depicted in the prime of their lives as young, healthy, and muscular.

It must be noted, that frontalism remained in place over the entirety of Pharaonic history, with only a two-decade period of realism interceding under Akhenaton's reign. Known as *Amarna* art, his juxtaposing style highlights his brave defiance from rigid conformity; and, given its fleeting nature, the inability of the status quo to accept change. It speaks volumes of about his mind, and hints to something so threatening to later rulers that it warranted the hasty destruction of his artefacts from history.

On my second visit, I chanced upon the area dedicated to this pharaoh. I was in awe. I don't know why I hadn't seen it on my first visit, perhaps because there really is so much to peruse. For some reason, which I will try to convey, I was fixated with him. When you see so many Egyptian art pieces over the many floors, you're initially enthralled, but after a while they do all seem very similar, and you get a small sense of 'seen one, seen 'em all'. Until you enter Akhenaton's area.

His presentation contrasts strikingly to that of his own son Tutankhamen, who reverted to the original art style for his portraiture. I can vividly recall when I turned around and saw the first statue of him. I was instantly struck by his beauty and strangeness in one moment. The masons for his statues were total masters of their art. In bare stone, for every single one, there was a subtle gentleness and wisdom in his face that no Greek sculpture or Michelangelo's *David* comes close to. With no colour, you can still see the softness of his character and unassuming power in every detail. Peculiarly distinct from regular Egyptian art, he has a sinuous quality to his upper body, in his shoulders and arms, yet wide voluptuous shaped hips like a woman. Regardless of these distortions – he is beautiful.

If you're aware of what you're looking for when interpreting art, there's so much information to be garnered. It did not occur to me until a decade later, having taught critical thinking in history classes, that *Amarna* art varied in many more ways than just the distortions of this King's body and facial structures. I became aware that he was the only pharaoh whose wall reliefs and paintings had him placed equally in scale and position with his family. Akhenaton was displayed symmetrically with his wife Nefertiti, and with him affectionately kissing and holding his daughters. All other pharaohs were captured with hunting or war scenes, leaving a legacy for us to presume they were powerful men and formidable leaders. Even the enigmatic Queen Hatshepsut resorted to representing herself as a man, with the recognisable extended beard piece in her statues and wall reliefs, as if making herself masculine was more desirable and acceptable to the observers.

Many historians hypothesise Akhenaton was depicted like this because he had a birth or genetic defect. Comparatively, his wife was presented very lifelike in terms of her appearance. So why present himself so markedly different, or not make himself more manly as other pharaohs had? This suggests to me that perhaps it's either for metaphorical reasons, to draw attention to feminine qualities he seems to have valued, contrary to Hatshepsut who had masculinised herself, or that he quite literally was ill-formed and unashamed of it. If the former was the intention, that of feminine likeness for veneration, this does not explain his unusually shaped face. Similarly, his daughter's busts (skull and shoulder sculptures) were carved with enormously elongated skulls, quite unnatural compared to busts of earlier or later royal representations.

If we compare Akhenaton's face to Nefertiti's proportionately human-shaped head, it is not unnatural to wonder if he was perhaps not of this world. His chin is very long and narrow, his eyes exaggeratedly wide, and his cheek bones high set and prominent. Keeping in mind his wife was presented as any ordinary woman we'd see today; one is compelled to wonder.

Interestingly, I stumbled on a scientific exploration of his DNA by Europeans who were curious to understand he and Tutankhamun's genetics. Quite unexpectedly, the scientists found they were of the haplogroup shared by 70% of the United Kingdom who were Celts, and startlingly, not of Arabic ancestry. From their investigation, they further discovered that less than 1% of present Egyptians had Celtic genes to confirm that both Pharaoh's DNA were definitively not of this heritage. This means these Pharaohs from 3,500 years ago were Caucasian men from an undiscovered region of the time, and who were not merely recorded as traveling merchants – but as Kings of great renown. How would academics explain that away, if not by some otherworldly origin?

The awe felt when I first discovered him was much deeper than simply marvelling at odd depictions of a unique Pharaoh. His very tall statues and sculpted busts are truly captivating; although I couldn't explain why they affected me on such a soul level, until I stumbled on a text about him a few years later. I loved browsing esoteric shops over the decades, and as I regularly did not have the money to buy, I was content with just absorbing the expansive feeling these shops gave me. I hadn't mastered the art of manifesting, as I'd gotten used to being broke, much like someone would get used to being burnt in hell after a while. Enlightenment was still just an air of excitement outside of me, and not yet taken home.

On one occasion, I saw the book *Akhenaton: The Extra-terrestrial King*, by Daniel Blair Stewart. The subject of Akhenaton with the word extra-terrestrial grabbed my attention. I could normally talk myself out of spending, but there was no way I could leave this behind. To this day, it has to be one of the best books I've ever read. Without spoiling its beautiful story, and that of the author and his reasons for writing it, I will highlight one of the interesting details I found in there. It included that only specific people were able to witness UFOs, despite being in full view. This helped me shape an understanding around why the skimming gold disk and the illuminated diamond didn't cause road chaos, or initiate people pulling over and jumping out of their cars. In the text, it described very simply that only those who were meant to see the craft were able to see it. In there, a character who gazed upon an obvious and distinct UFO in the clear of day, wondered why others were going about their business without distraction by its presence. If this phenomenon is true, then this presents questions about how the intelligently controlled spaceships can uncloak for some individuals and not for all.

Presuming this is a possibility, then their capacity to manipulate visibility to certain individuals offers an astounding degree of technological advancement. Would this mean the occupants are able to singularly and remotely control our area of the brain to see it, or simultaneously close all other passers-by to not? Either way, this technology, or their will over matter, is vastly evolved compared to our own.

During this period of my life, a decade into studying personal enlightenment, I'd acquired quite a few disciplines to focus my mind for changing my life. One thing about Ramtha's school that I'll reiterate – it's all about us and our will and effort to use our brains to make magic happen. The school requires an active participatory involvement, and overcoming our gripes, fears, and emotional baggage, means it isn't for the lazy. Basically, we'll get the results according to how much we dedicate ourselves to the work. In my earlier years, I did the disciplines like a religious person prays; much like an obedient daughter really – which is why I didn't have meaningful change. Like I've already said: I'm a slow learner.

My infinitesimally small understanding of the brain's true capacity, despite all the reading and studying Ram recommended about physics, and research around the brain, still didn't sink in. This true capability – for all of us – was not actualised until recent years, where I had the realisation that I had a tiny part in allowing the UFOs to appear. The following account will elaborate why I knew the miraculous was occurring as a result of the disciplines I was applying.

All disciplines require an understanding of the construction of matter from energy into atoms. Simply put: threads of energy, or waves of frequency, slow down to condense into sub-atomic particles, then into atoms – solid matter. This wave to particle principle peculiarly only forms when it's being observed. Hence the Buddhist question: if a tree falls alone in the forest does it make a sound? If being observed by anyone forms reality – then that makes us God-like.

Christian text corroborates this by including that Jesus said even the lesser of us can do what he did, and greater. That's worth deliberating. Essentially, then, he claimed that even people who were the scum of the Earth had the same potential as him and could do more than raise the dead and walk on water. If you give the text any credit of reliability, despite severe editing and the enormous amount of gospels left out, this should be the most ground-breaking concept in existence. And it should've been for me too – years ago.

Before progressing, it is worth interjecting that just being told we can manifest, or shape reality, is an empty concept. Learning a technique to achieve tangible results isn't sustainable unless we know the 'why' behind how it works. Curious people attend ashrams, or new-age teachers and gurus, to learn practices for personal freedom or healing, but the interest wanes and the emotional gains are brief – unless we've got the science behind it. Such a narrow path just isn't enough for me. We can only 'believe' something for so long; and humans' tendency to get bored or doubt why it hasn't happened, soon lose the gusto in keeping it up. This is why knowing the current research on energy, physics, biology, and the like, provide more than belief, and enters the realm of participatory knowledge.

All disciplines require attentive focus on a singular idea to affect the field. One of those, called the Grid®, Ram described as a powerful voodoo, and for some reason, his use of these terms resonated with me above other disciplines. This one was to become my most demonstrable technique used.

During one retreat, we'd had an in-depth teaching about the grid that conceptualised how we can create matter, or reality, by its use. I'm not qualified to teach it accurately, but for expressive purposes, it can be described as a realm where infinite energy streams exist. This first semblance of visible energy emerging from the void carry information that form the patterns or blueprints of the material world. We learnt how different frequencies of energy exist in the seen and unseen world, and which one with its corresponding colour is needed to manipulate the grid into materialising our focused intent.

As usual, every morning my phone alarm was set to indicate it was time to get up. Back then, my phone wasn't a smartphone and I had the same sound for the alarm and phone calls. We were asked to be outside at 5:30am to do the grid discipline and being dark during winter I'd set mine earlier. I knew I'd be desperate for a warm coffee before I went out to sit for half an hour in the cold!

On one of these occasions, as I pressed the alarm off – startled and disoriented from the sound waking me – I sat up and saw something amazing. It was only for a few moments, but long enough for me to be struck by it its beauty. The darkened room was filled with multi-directional streams of fine, blue-silver threads. A few seconds after seeing the filaments of energy, they spun simultaneously anti-clockwise, forming a detailed, circular geometric pattern – much like an intricate crop circle with many right-angled, connecting lines. It was so beautiful, and I marvelled over it for a moment before I remembered I had to get up to do the grid, where it instantly disappeared.

I've had trouble not rushing most of my adult life, always sensing a feeling of urgency brought about by trying to squeeze in too much work. As such, I rushed down the hall to the kitchen and turned the kettle on. Leaning against the bench, I caught a glimpse of the clock on the wall. "What the fuck?!". It was five minutes to midnight! I was momentarily confused before realising it must've been a phone call, and I'd inadvertently hung up on the caller. I thought it must be an emergency to be calling in the middle of the night, so I quickly ran to my room and returned the call, which was from my husband. He answered in a voice that was groggy and woken from a heavy sleep. "Sorry", I said. "I thought it was my alarm and I pressed stop". He replied that that was hours ago, around nine o'clock. I insisted it was only a minute ago, and he had no idea what I was talking about. He said it was just to see how I was going, and the call ended pretty quickly. I checked the call log. Holy shit! The incoming call was three hours before.

I kid you not – it was only about three minutes between the call that I mistook for an alarm, going to the kitchen, then running back to return the call I'd hung up on. This vision of the grid concept was no doubt some serious kind of voodoo!

And it was this discipline that would be a game changer for seeing the miraculous thereafter.

CHAPTER SEVEN

The Boomerang

For the first few years of having my Egyptian husband live with us in Australia, I found myself frequently annoyed at his constant need to have TV on when he was home. My daughter and I had been regular readers, or we tended to spend time chatting, drawing, and other activities that weren't filled with constant noise and commercials that screamed at us every ten minutes. Funny how adversity bumps us in the right direction: we got used to avoiding it by going out for an hour or two every night to do our disciplines, in the small park across the road. It was the perfect location, peppered with large haunting trees that blocked the streetlights, and our chihuahua got to potter around while we lay on the grass, looking at the sky doing the Grid.

One night, we saw a huge silver boomerang float silently above us in a gap between the clouds, exactly in our gaze. Together we both said, "Did you see that?!". It was literally a perfect boomerang; not to be confused with a plane – there was nothing wrong with our eyes!

This location, on the southern end of the Gold Coast, happened to be situated at the northern side of the international airport, near where my first gold disk had flung over our car. The airstrip was about five hundred metres away, and the sound of roaring planes descending is unmistakable. Planes landing from the northern end meant they were low enough to rip open our ear drums and see the lights across its belly and wings. This was a non-descript silver boomerang floating across our view. No tail or nose of a traditional plane – just the pointed end of the chevron shape moving forwards, and the diagonal sides angled backwards. The width of the wings were largely consistent through to the ends, narrowing only slightly, where they were rounded.

There was sufficient light from the suburb, airport, and highway only fifty metres from us, which allowed an unhindered view of it. No lights were emanating from the craft, and its metal surface was plainly visible. On this occasion, however, the craft was higher above us – I'm guessing one or two hundred metres – and there was no insignia on its underside to speak of, as one would normally see on planes overhead at this altitude.

My daughter and I had also started taking our cheap quality digital camera out, capturing orbs and other anomalies on the memory card. The cheaper and older the model the better the images caught, as those ones didn't have superior filters to block out infrared and other frequencies. We would get incredible images, mostly an array of faces in varying colours, but I will share one relevant to the topic of this book.

I'd seen some mind-blowing photos caught by Michael Ledwith, former academic in Irish universities, and catholic representative to Pope John Paul II. As a former Dean of Theology, he'd studied Ramtha's teachings, and many others, and was impressed with the school and its focus on students' application of disciplines in opening the brain.

On one retreat, he showed us several consecutive images of what appeared to be an object that was angular in shape, and moving closer to inspect him in each consecutive image. It appeared in the photo to be ghostly coloured, transparent and glowing; and Michael assured us that others present could not see it with their eyes. From adequate training, he demonstrated in the photographs that he could see it with his naked eye and had his hands on either side of it in the air to show this capability.

On one occasion, we were also able to see images taken in quick succession from our balcony of an angular object. It appeared to move from across the neighbour's yard towards us, until it was within arm's length. Like Michael's images, the object appeared transparent with light emanating from it, yet it was not visible to our eyes for either my daughter, myself, or my cousin present. It proved to us that extra-terrestrial surveillance is not limited to quietly observing craft. Unfortunately, when our laptop was getting repaired, my then husband didn't save the images and the thousands we had amassed were wiped away.

One night, my Turkish friend came with me while I was doing the grid in my backyard. I hadn't explained the scientific principles of the process, and instead suggested we were just meditating with our eyes open. We sat quietly in a cross-legged posture, both facing the trees where I usually did my disciplines across the road. The direction minimised the streetlights coming from the nearby highway, and this side of the backyard didn't face onto brick walls of the surrounding unit complexes.

When we do the grid, we're focussing at a relatively short distance in the air, and the objects behind it – including stars – become blurred. This is because we're holding an image in our mind instead of seeing what's in our view; and it's preferably done gazing upwards towards an open sky.

Quite often, and even now, I am distracted by moving planes with their flashing lights and need to refocus. Regularly, I'll see an instant acceleration of white or gold light, and more often than not, these occur directly in my line of vision. Such occurrences are distinguishable from falling stars that enter the atmosphere and diminish, scattering fragments in its downward cascade, and I denote them as being UFOs. The propulsive jettisons also don't appear to have a slow start that increase in velocity like planes, but appear to instantaneously take off from a still position and maintain a horizontal trajectory. The rapid interaction of their movement against the particles in the atmosphere obviously causes enough friction to create a brilliant light stream that I estimate as being a kilometre long. These little encounters definitely capture my attention, and I generally have a little smile before refocusing.

On the night with my friend, I instead gazed directly in front of me at the treetops across the road. I think I lowered my gaze on this occasion to extend the time I could sit without arching my head up, as I'd normally be laying back on the grass. Neither of us talked, naturally, and I was engaged in the discipline to the best of my untrained and scattered mind's ability. I must have been doing something right, however, for what happened next.

Usually, when something distracts me it's instantaneous, from what is otherwise supposed to be a trance-like state. On this occasion, however, I wasn't distracted but instead phased gently out of focus, maintaining my gaze in the exact position. When someone says they had a moment of being stunned and of not knowing what's going on, they mean it! Right in my line of vision was the silver boomerang again. It didn't enter my view from one side, it was *just there*. Stationary and silent.

This time it was about thirty to forty metres from me, and close enough that I could approximate the width to that of a regular sized, free-standing suburban home. No lights, windows or visible portals, just seamless silver sheeting across its surface. It was low enough that I could see its upper body, which was not high to speak of, but predominantly flattened from one side to the other. I couldn't see its underbelly because of its position directly in front of me, and the streetlight right next to it illuminated its upper surface. There were no striations on the wings, if you can call them that, because it didn't have a body where wings attach. Just a perfectly smooth, metal boomerang. Although it was flat on the top, I could detect it had a gradual thickening towards its centre, creating some space for occupants in the middle – but certainly, not much. It was positioned from the side, but sufficiently angled that I could see its breadth across both wings. If I was to estimate the cabin height, I'd say no more than a metre and a half, so whoever was in there was obviously seated or very small.

After about ten seconds of gazing, a row of lights lit up simultaneously across the entire upper back edge of the chevron, and – voom! It instantly accelerated away from us at an infinitesimal speed over the houses in its front, with a gold stream of light at its rear. Again, utterly silent, and no displacement of air. Unbelievable!

I immediately became aware that my friend was still sitting silent and unresponsive. I turned my head slightly, curious to understand why she'd remained unphased at such a remarkable event, and noticed my friend was gazing directly as I had been, towards the same trees. I noted that her attention was strangely uninterrupted. She had not seen it. I gently turned my eyes forward and deliberated about asking her, when clearly, she had not seen the brilliant display.

It was puzzling to me that the power up of lights and intense tail stream was not seen by her. I decided to say nothing. If she was looking in the same vicinity as me, she was not going to believe me. Later that night, my daughter called me in. "Mum", she said, "I saw the hugest UFO. It was so big it completely blocked out my view in the window".

I could not doubt her, after all, I'd just had an unearthly boomerang stationed in front of me! She was around twelve then, and she said it was so huge she got frightened. This was very interesting. Her bedroom was on the first floor to the right where I'd been sitting, and if it was so huge then why didn't I see that with my own? If incredibly advanced beings are able to control the separate individual minds of onlookers, then we're talking absolute masters over matter – and consciousness. It never occurred to me then why I wasn't privy to seeing the monster my daughter described. Was it so big that they knew I'd probably lose my shit in shock? Did they deduce that this enormity would've frightened me and decide that a smaller reconnaissance vehicle would be better received?

Over the course of several months of writing I've repeatedly asked my daughter, now thirty, to sit and describe the huge manifestation she saw. She never responded, and I suspect she was reticent to be involved in outing herself about this marvel. I persevered, as a mother ship was worthy of pursuing, and I wanted to garner the full extent of its size for myself and readers. Since I didn't see it, I had no details to convey – and I wanted them!

It wasn't until later, more accurately – over many years, that I wondered about the enormity of these other-worldly events. I still find it difficult to process properly that I've had tangible UFOs near to me. It raises so many questions, generally the same ones again and again. Who the bloody hell is in them?! What do they look like? Do they know me, or was it the interaction of the field from my discipline that provided them a rip in space to this world? Surely craft that could materialise in my gaze didn't need my input on the field to permit their entry. These pilots were Masters of it.

If these beings were able to know where I was, and at what time, then their capabilities were beyond time and space. Their technologies must be billions of years ahead of ours. Remembering one thing too: if they can create these technologies then they must have the consciousness to design them. Ramtha offers many insights into different races, and I recall one amazing story as an example of their expansive minds.

He described how one such race was so spiritually advanced that they'd overcome death. I'm sure this must be the case for countless races, whether it be immortality on a physical level using technology, or complete conscious mastery over matter itself. He explained that if they were creating a new design of something, such as a spaceship, and something went wrong and they exploded to smithereens, they'd be instantly standing on the ground, casually discussing what didn't work. It makes sense, then, that if we understand the quantum field of all reality, then dying in flesh and blood bodies is a no thing; and mastery over time, space and matter means just pressing rewind consciously, and returning to where we were standing before we blew up!

This then begs the question: why would beings of this magnitude in consciousness need craft at all? Why not just travel via the mind in the quantum field? I can only imagine that when races no longer need to perform perpetual labour, as we do here, then the natural inclination is always to learn and create, push boundaries, and extract new ideas from the void. Having vehicles may also be a way of demonstrating to us that there is a bigger, fuller universe out there.

If we look at nature, we can see that it is always evolving, or more accurately – creating. Flora always adapts to new conditions, albeit slowly, and finds new ways to perpetuate itself when conditions are no longer conducive to its survival. For human beings, being creative seems a natural desire that motivates us too. We get together and come up with new ideas, figure out ways of doing things faster or more efficiently. Perhaps interacting together with others in a physical form is still desirable when one has mastered time and space – providing a platform for engaging face to face with others of their ilk.

This suggests, then, that having a vehicle to share a 'space' with others of like mind and mastery, also offers them a singular point in time to engage with us on earth. If they'd suddenly materialised in front of me in their distinctly different forms, I most certainly would have crapped myself. Having a craft appear is probably the least confronting way of showing us earthlings there's infinite others out there; and I surmise when we've got knowledge of how to interact with the field, then we've demonstrated steps of evolution that is of interest to them, and they'll show up in the least confronting way.

For me, the ones that paused and stayed present with my daughter and I seemed personal. I couldn't reduce their presence to just me creating an entry point for multi-dimensional craft to enter, although this idea lingered for some years. They were present with my daughters and me, and they knew we were present with them.

CHAPTER EIGHT

The Owl

If you've ever watched the film adaptation of Whitley Streiber's book *Communion* you'd get the impression that extra-terrestrial beings are terrifying. When I watched that film for the first time, I was convinced every single element of crazy shit that happened in there must be true. There's no way anyone would risk their reputation, career, family, or relationships, for something this far out. I can only imagine what coming out with these details put him through, and I doubt any amount of money would motivate someone to make such things up, only to lose everything.

I hadn't seen the film during my few years living across the road from the park, but I had seen the film *Fire in the Sky*, a recount of Travis Walton's abduction experience. A far swing from the friendly little beings who held Richard Dreyfuss's hand as they guided him onboard in *Close Encounters of the Third Kind* – these creatures were terrifying. Besides being what we'd define here as ugly, they were completely devoid of compassion when taking people up, performing varying kinds of invasive procedures, and for some in the craft, left to rot onboard.

This kind of propaganda is no doubt going to imprint abject terror into anyone's mind here on earth. And, remembering everyone's

Chapter 8: The Owl

inherent ability to manipulate the field, we are literally going to push close encounters, of any kind, far out of the realm of possibility and experience after viewing this. Perhaps this is deliberate.

One night, I went as usual with my chihuahua to the park for focus, and to allow him to do his business before being stuck in the unit for the night. As you enter the park, there's a single roomed electricity block that is brightly lit by a streetlight, and it also had a fluorescent light above an access door for visibility. To the side, about ten metres away, is a concrete footpath that also has lighting for people to cross over a storm drain to the next street. All of these lights I'd avoid by going around the little building, and into the slightly forested area behind.

I'd never do the grid in bright light, as you can't see the sky very well, and dark settings are very conducive to chemicals the brain produces for alternate states. The cascade of neurotransmitters is normally used for the brain to send abstract instructions to the body for healing when we sleep, but they also allow interaction with the field in mystical ways. We can still achieve this when used in the day with blindfolds on, and some disciplines are in fact done in the daylight, but in my experience the exposure to light and the serotonin it produces doesn't quite shift me into states as quickly. We are already starting to enter into a dreamlike state when nightfall begins, and doing disciplines during the night becomes particularly trippy and cool.

As usual, I stepped onto the well-lit grass to head towards the treed area where there was also an open space to lay and face upwards at the sky. Glancing at the block I was approaching; I saw something I'd never seen in my life. A giant owl was standing on the grass in full light. I wondered why it would be exposing itself to predators by standing on the ground, as they are secretive birds of prey that remain quietly observant in the trees.

My little dog was sniffing ahead of me on the grass, and suddenly stopped and stared at it. Its presence near him was obviously intriguing to him too, and he quickly tip toed up closer to investigate. I didn't want to frighten the owl off, as it was such a lovely and unusual occurrence to see, so I tried whispering and gesturing my dog to come back. He was a curious little thing who ignored me, so I had to creep stealthily to the giant bird to get him, in case it was startled back up to the trees.

After collecting the dog, I slowly withdrew and passed at a distance I felt would not make it fly away. It naturally maintained eye contact with me for its own safety – and I kept my eyes on it too – as it isn't often you get to see a giant owl standing there on the open grass!

Sometime after, my cousin came alone to stay for a holiday from Victoria. Everyone comes to the Gold Coast for holidays, especially when there's free accommodation, and why not? It's beautiful. It wasn't the first time she'd come up to visit, as once she'd stayed in a resort overlooking the beach with her family. On that occasion she was still a teenager, and our family went along for an outdoor BBQ one night during their stay.

The resort BBQ area was on the rooftop, where the spa was also located. While we soaked, I brought up the idea of UFOs during our conversation, and she was sceptical. I was a bit more open about convincing her than I was to friends and outsiders, as this kind of conversation is predictably going to be one of your last with them, for obvious reasons.

As I was describing my UFO experiences, where I recall she was looking blankly at me, waiting politely for me to shut up, I spotted something sailing southbound at eye level, over the darkened sea. Now, again, this location is the descending zone for landing planes, and the planes here are so low and close as to hear their engines and see their logos clearly. That said, there are very few flights descending at night because it's a residential area.

In total silence, approximately 300–400 hundred metres from us, something was floating past, pulsating as it did. By pulsating,

Chapter 8: The Owl

I mean it had an unbroken light around its perimeter that radiated slowly off and on in a rhythmic way. Regular plane lights stay consistently on in some parts, and flash in others. Helicopters are also noisy and have similar lighting. This object had no sound, and a singular light spanning from front to rear glowed every other second.

"Look!", I called, as I gestured with my hand towards it. "It's a UFO!". We just stared for a few moments to take it in. I couldn't describe its shape very easily because of the distance, and because the pulsating light was momentary. On this occasion, it didn't pause to watch us, only glided by silently and consistently. I laughed, and said how cool it was that it'd happened when my cousin wouldn't believe it until she'd seen it. The object was close enough to determine it was circular, as there didn't appear to be wings extended out to the sides as we would see on planes, nor a dorsal fin atop the rear. In fact, there were no extensions to speak of from any part. Awesome. She got confirmation immediately, and I was a little chuffed that they'd done that for us.

On her solo visit, I introduced her to our hobby of photographing orbs: the ghostly apparitions that appear as small, translucent circles. We can refute many orbs as being mist or condensation, but when we have blue ones with upward turned eyes, as an example among a myriad of clear facial features, there's no denying it. In fact, the more regularly you do it, the more comfortable beings become and allow themselves to be pictured. My daughter and I had one night where they were a little scant, and being an innocent, she called out, "Come out, we love you!", and just like that, the next picture was packed full of faces in different shapes and colours. Showing the sampling of images to my cousin impressed her, and surprisingly, terrified her.

I told her also about the huge owl I'd spotted on the grass across the road. Her occupation as an environmental scientist included tallying different species of wildlife near developments and road projects, and she was confident in her evaluation of my retelling.

"How big was it?", she asked.

"Oh, about two feet tall", I answered.

"We don't have owls that big in this country".

"Don't we? Well, I saw it, and Ezzy went straight up to it. So, he saw it too".

I can't recall if we discussed anymore about the owl, but I can recount how utterly frightened she was about going across the road to take pictures. It was so funny; I had tears rolling down my cheeks from laughing, as I pulled on her arms to let go of the railing and go downstairs. She would not budge, and we ended up doing our orb photos from the balcony. This was the occasion we caught the 'device', that in progressive pictures, travelled towards us.

I can't say definitively where I'd later heard about giant owls being seen by people who recounted alien abductions. I seem to recall Whitley Strieber's *Communion* including this, which I'd have to revisit to be sure, and I've watched many abductee documentaries to know this is a recurring theme. I can understand that externally controlling the human's mind to see owls may be a plausible way for abductees to see something less terrifying.

Alternatively, we may be creating our own image of them in our brain, and not they who are controlling our mind. Owls have dark upturned eyes, enhanced by distinctive rings to trap light at night, and this may instead be our way of constructing what we're seeing when it appears out of context or is unexpected. I remember in Central Park, New York, where I stood watching autumn leaves flitter about on the grass from the wind, when my friend asked me if I saw "them". "See what?", I asked. When he said tiny squirrels, I instantly saw the little things scurrying about where there'd been none a moment before. I'd never seen one in real life, and besides the odd cartoon as a kid, they were not in my head to conceptualise. Given that I'd had grey alien exposure in films, however, it's likely I could construct their appearance neurologically but would've carked it on the spot if I had. So, it would seem logical that it was mind control in my encounter.

Chapter 8: The Owl

To whatever reason we attribute to why people see owls with abductions is not of particular interest to me. It is the terror that such people recall under hypnosis that perturbs me. I must say, despite all of my other-worldly experiences, I'm not convinced about the authenticity of hypnosis in extracting these events. I've had it done once, and it didn't work. When watching people undergo this, they're screaming and moving erratically. I am cynical in my wondering as to why this doesn't wake them up. Don't take my word on this though, as I'm not a doctor, and perhaps it is very genuine.

More noteworthy is the alleged horror experienced by abductees. This is great marketing across a broad spread of the public for convincing us that aliens are cruel and worth avoiding. I have trouble with this persuasion for several reasons, as I don't believe these events are as nefarious as we're made to believe. Firstly, let's look at the terms we've become familiar with: *aliens* and *abduction*. The former has become conditioned in us to be associated with terror and annihilation if we recall films with this term in its title. The term also implies that these visitors are unwelcome when we consider its use for illegal migrants. Abduction, too, has sinister connotations. Abductors have hostages whose lives are at risk, and if they're fortunate enough to be returned alive, have endured wakeful moments of real terror.

If we are to believe extra-terrestrial beings taking humans onboard have malevolent intentions, why do they bother to blot out horrifying memories? This seems a rather compassionate thing to me. And why bother to return us to our original location unconscious, if not to prevent us from having the trauma of our experience? They could just eject us into space after they've taken their tissue samples and not give a damn about us. We may even be slightly obnoxious and consider ourselves lucky they chose us for their sampling or reproductive cells. After all, they must have criteria for selection if they are needing something, and our body fits the bill.

Travis Walton is an excellent case where the media has turned his experience into a horror movie. For all intents and purposes, it was a very well-made movie for the early days in creating life-like horror in space, using simple computerised special effects. The rotting, decomposed bodies on board, and the demonic beings drilling his eyes certainly scared the hell out of me in the early '90s.

If you're reading this, you may already know Mr Walton has completely denigrated the evil representation of his abductors. To quickly recap for those who aren't familiar, he says his experience was nothing evil at all. He believes he was accidentally affected by the energy emanating from the craft, as he was beneath it when it slowly rose, throwing him like one would experience a lightning strike or electrocution. Walton states that upon his awakening, the little greys, as they are termed, stood back from him when he attempted to get up from the examination table. He held an object up to defend himself, and after a few moments of looking placidly at him, they quietly left the room. Doesn't sound like they were intent on overpowering him at all, which I'm sure they were technologically capable of.

As he wandered around the craft to get out, human looking beings escorted him elsewhere, and gently lay him down to be made unconscious. He recounts that they looked concerned, and he is adamant they were taking care of him. Like others, he was returned to his original location, in fact right next to a street phone to ring for help! Surely, if they hadn't have cared for this human, they could've left him where the event occurred, which may have killed him, or they could have dumped him anywhere on earth after they'd had him. I don't buy the cruel imagery anymore, and certainly don't subscribe to scare mongering by the media.

For me, I always had the sense of benevolence, because on most occasions I was applying spiritual disciplines when they came. They didn't appear during family arguments or other disturbances – only during still and wonderous endeavours of me trying to open by brain

Chapter 8: The Owl

for a better life. In my mind, the practice must have been so worthy that they wanted to give me confirmation. What better confirmation could you get than real-life, tangible craft silently with you? A couple of craft came more than once, such as the boomerang, a couple were close enough to throw a ball at, and some appeared when I wasn't actively doing a discipline at all. Overall, though, I think over a dozen occasions is pretty good statistical evidence I was applying a skill everyone could benefit from: using my brain to manipulate reality.

CHAPTER NINE

The Green Rockets

During the first few years with my husband, there were instances where his addictions emerged. I'd also lost my relationship with my dad over marrying him, as he lived minutes away and never made any attempt to contact me or his granddaughter. This hurt so much, and I was too ashamed to admit to myself he may have been right in his warnings. Originally, I thought my dad's attempts to impede our move to Egypt was a bigoted one, and I hoped to eventually prove him wrong. Instead, situations and events showed otherwise.

There were always things that needed explaining. Like my tin of about $1500, saved for my next retreat, and my daughter's $400 birthday savings disappearing in one day. "It was the neighbour", according to my husband, as he'd allegedly seen him leaving our house once (yeah, right). There were also several occasions where he'd tell me a friend wanted to visit the brothels; and when I questioned why one from the mosque would do that when he had his beautiful wife, he replied, "She doesn't count". He'd said that just a bit too easily.

Writing these things still disturb me, because I haven't yet fully processed that the anger generated is really for my own choices. Yet,

Chapter 9: The Green Rockets

despite what I ended up passing through, I never gave up my disciplines, even when trailer loads of crap were hitting the fan.

My intent then was to make sure everything looked hunky dory to my family. My dad and brother had excellent wins with real estate, and I'd forgone many opportunities with my dad to buy in a few years prior. I was again pregnant, and yes, it was against my better judgment. I hoped having a baby might make him more dedicated to me and stop pulling all-nighters watching porn. With these things in mind, I ensured we bought a house to present a story that everything was working out right. It was my first home purchase, much later than friends and colleagues I'd had, who weren't delayed by tangential, fanciful ideas like me.

After moving in, I noticed pretty quickly that there was a nut job across the road, and I warned my husband to stay away from him. My daughter and I regularly stood behind vertical blinds like meerkats, watching him carry on. He'd scream derogatory comments to other neighbours almost every night, and as my husband had a shitty factory-hand job at nights, he missed the theatrics. I later found out he'd ignored me, and our safety, and I discovered the two were swapping files of hardcore porn during the day. The guy's surname was Blood. This was quite befitting for him really, as we were to find out.

One night there was a knock at the front door. As soon as I opened it, I saw our neighbour standing there covered in blood, still wet all over his front. He was also completely naked, except for a threadbare, tiny towel he was holding in place over his groin. His pupils were unnaturally large, so I assumed he was off his tree on something, and he asked to come in and hang out. I immediately thought he'd murdered his mum, to account for so much blood, as I couldn't see any injuries. I was terrified, but didn't show it.

After apologising that he couldn't, and politely closing the door – it was on. And it would be on for the next three years, with a brick through my windscreen, four arrests, two court appearances, and a three-month jail term. When I called the police that first night, because he was screaming insults and banging on my front door, the emergency operator thought I was pranking him when I said his surname was Blood.

The relentless torment occurred almost daily. Obscene insults shouted across the street for my daughter and neighbours to hear. At the time, it wasn't his cruel descriptions of me that disturbed me – his actions spoke louder than words in this long, drawn out assault.

On one occasion, my eldest daughter and I managed to record him going off at us from across the street for the whole neighbourhood to hear. We had a quiet giggle from behind the bushes, as this was his most crude, offensive outburst we'd caught, and we knew the cops would have to respond. When they arrived, one of the two was an Amazonian woman, beautiful and muscular, standing above the other man in stature. As she sat in our lounge listening to the lunatic on my phone, I noted her manicured red nails. She was feminine and friendly, and elaborated how she hadn't slept in three nights, with only an hour when she returned home to mind her toddlers, as a single mum. What a champion.

As she spoke, there was a thunderous banging on the front door, accompanied with hysterical screams yelling, "Police harassment!", and threats of suing for such.

"Who's that?!", she asked, with a genuinely puzzled look.

"That's him", we smiled, knowing what a fucking weirdo he must've seemed.

"Sounds like an old woman!".

"I know", we replied, smirking.

He had that outdated eighties appearance about him; and he had an effeminate voice that made his overall demeanour quite unusual, in contrast to his threatening behaviours. Despite the gravity of it all, my daughter and I had an excited feeling arising from it, especially that he'd come right over with police present and started carrying on. We knew it would be a bit of comic relief, even if not long lasting.

We both sat out in the dark, listening silently as they knocked on his front door, where he'd gone for refuge. Not a second passed

Chapter 9: The Green Rockets

after he opened it did the entertainment begin. There was smashing of bodies on walls and floors, and furniture being upended from one end of the house to the other. He had a timber floor, so the sound carried fluently across the street. Every few seconds we'd hear the guy banged to the floor, squealing like a stuck pig. It was awesome; and that gorgeous feminine warrior was obviously doing well on no sleep.

After the drama of his arrest, she called me for an update. She said it was the most bizarre thing she'd ever seen. His mum was painting on a canvas during the entire ordeal, and not once did she put her brush down to enquire, encourage him, or anything, regarding the event. She carried on painting like a messed-up, old Hollywood actress from a horror movie, oblivious and unspoken, from start to finish.

Every time he was arrested, he'd be released and resume the next day. When dozens of calls to police resulted in them chit chatting casually and apologising for disturbing him, if I didn't manage to record any evidence, I decided to send some audio files to our TV show *A Current Affair*. They were clearly gold to them, so they came within days, but the presenter was a familiar face to Australians, and Mr Blood behaved. Towards the end of the three years, I had momentary ideations about ways I'd murder and dispose of his body – it was that bad – for my daughter too, who was finishing her last years of high school.

I pushed on and never gave up my focus, but I'll admit it wasn't easy. My husband continued to have too many things he needed to explain, including a 'wrongful' conviction of soliciting an undercover cop disguised as a prostitute, and an unfamiliar toothbrush in my ensuite after I'd been out with our only car. Another more notable incident he couldn't explain, was a call to Egypt I made when he was there after his mum was diagnosed with cancer. My call was received with a fifteen-minute audible sex session, where it'd obviously meant to be disconnected instead of answered. I was in too deep with a mortgage and a toddler by then, and I had to believe the lies. I didn't know how to end it, and I was scared of what he'd do if I did.

Growing up as an air force kid, I'd had many opportunities to see fighter jets soar overhead, usually on Christmas parties or other celebrations. I also remember being taken as a little one onto the runway of the air base to a roaring Hercules. The engines were fired up so incredibly loud, and it was unbelievably exciting. I was lifted to the top of the plane and passed by my dad to other young men through an open hatch. I must've been very small, maybe four or five, and I never forgot how awesome this experience was. Sometimes here on the Gold Coast jets zoom quite low across the water at the beach, and their ripping blast tears through you as it lags a few seconds behind. It's the intensity of the sound that elicits the feeling of exhilaration, and I'm sure it's a universal experience. So, what do we do with this visual when there's no sound?

One night I was focusing alone under the stars, quite distractedly, and not from you-know-who. Mozzies, as we term them here, were horrendous in this southerly facing position, just over the border into New South Wales. The house was perched up on a small mountain with unobstructed views of the night sky. It faced away from the Gold Coast, so offered an array of stars not normally visible facing the eastern side. I could describe it as feeling elevated into space, making it perfect for doing the grid discipline.

Let me say that my focus was never UFOs. I can't say I recall what I was focusing on, but with the immense dramas always occurring, it was no doubt on having a life free of them. In this period, I was working full-time with a toddler, managing the landscaped yards on my own, and was forced to start getting up at 4:00am to get all the work done. I used to convince myself how hard my husband had it working until after midnight in a lousy job, so took it upon

Chapter 9: The Green Rockets

myself to do everything. Like my dad, I thought if I did more for him, he'd love me.

As I held my gaze, and did my darndest to hold one image, the spectacular occurred. Sitting there with incessant needles pricking me through the bedsheet I was wrapped in, I obviously must've been able to affect the quantum field with my meagre effort. Directly in my gaze, a green, glowing rocket pierced our dimension. It didn't enter from one side – I saw it come through nose first *into* our 'space'.

It was a typical rocket shape, with a flattened underside, narrow pointed front end, and a triangular upper dorsal at the rear. I couldn't see wings like an ordinary jet, and as it raced across to my right and leaned elliptically to pass, I still could not see wings at its sides. It appeared isosceles in shape, with the two sides being longer than the back side. There were no lights at all, except the entirety of the craft had an iridescent grass-green haze over the skin. I'd say it was about two hundred metres in front of me, at a 45-degree height, but it lowered to my altitude as it swerved around my small mountainside. I couldn't describe the colour of the rocket because of the rich, green glow it emitted, except that it was dark coloured, and I can say it was slightly smaller than a fighter jet we see here. And there was zero sound. Zero.

In my stunned gaze, I said out loud what any person would if this were to occur for them, "FUUUUUUUCK!!". As it disappeared out of sight, I wished that my eldest daughter had been there, as she often joined me in focus. Just as I had that thought, and returned my gaze to the original point, another pierced into this dimension from the exact spot the first had. Another absolute wonder. It was a duplicate of the first, and I was aghast at my luck at having two in one instance. Then, suddenly, a third pierced through! I use the word 'pierced' to reiterate the visual, because it entered into our atmosphere via the spot in the sky. The third was also identical to the first pair, and all silently followed the same trajectory out of view.

My god! Three rockets using my focus point to penetrate this world. On this occasion they weren't stopping to say 'Hi', but they gave me the gift of entering in my focus space, and that was magic enough. This spoke volumes of my practice – and the grid discipline. I can't say that it's hard to keep focussing after the craft appear – because I don't continue focussing at all. I'm so electrified and floaty from the experience.

This total wonder ignited the same questions in my mind that I always had afterwards. Did they enter that spot *because* of my discipline? I did think that about this particular event over the years, after all, they'd used my narrow gaze to enter into, but I was also rather certain craft of that calibre didn't need any piddly human effort to enter – they're eons ahead in technology. They did put me in their mind, however, otherwise why would they bother entering in through my miniscule spot of the night sky? They knew I was there at that moment in time, which means they must have known who I was and what I was doing.

CHAPTER TEN

The Sonic Boom

The disciplines are so called for several purposeful reasons. They're not meditating, nor mindfulness, or breathwork. They are determined focus on an image that the author has imbued with information, long enough for the brain to hardwire and manifest from the quantum field to experience.

To generalise, when we meditate our attention is on the body, such as breathing, or feelings we conjure to find more peace and presence. We're also endeavouring to slow our breathing down to quiet the sympathetic nervous system, out of fight, flight, or freeze. The result should be a move into the parasympathetic system, that of rest and digest. The disciplines therefore are entirely different. They are for creation. And the struggle to hold a singular idea is difficult – hence the term discipline – and their application for stuck humans requires extended periods, if we want results.

The action of holding an image resembles the process the brain undergoes when we have conversations, where information is contained in a visual representation. For example, when reading this text, we are simultaneously constructing a picture of what is being described. Similarly, when our body dreams during the repair stage of sleep, our brain doesn't send verbal instructions to the body, it sends imagery. Imagine if it said, "Ok knee, grow cartilage behind the patella". It just doesn't; it's an abstract collage of images that contains all the necessary details. This applies to its use in focus also. We don't need to explain to ourselves what to do with the image, we already know, and thus the brain does too.

Another aspect that needs clarifying, in order to understand directed focus, is why emotions have no part in creation. I've heard mindfulness practitioners advise to feel what we want in our life, but is this only drawing on the already familiar responses we've lived thus far, much like academics postulating their hypotheses within the parameters of their understanding I referred to earlier? If we unpack the brain a little, we can understand why feeling something in the body, to stimulate happiness or freedom from worry etcetera, may alleviate our symptoms for a while – and possibly hardwire the experience to some degree eventually – it isn't manifesting or healing permanently.

Consider very simply that the brain has three parts. The top portion, extending from our forehead over to our crown, is the *thinking* part. The inner, mid-section is our *feeling* area, and the base at the rear is our *knowing* part. Whilst this is a crude simplification, you can get the gist of the areas.

Our very earliest ancestors had no prominent forehead, similar in shape to monkeys today. This was due to the limited sized thinking part. Instead, the earliest hominids relied on instinct, hormones and emotions, to prompt them for survival. Hence, reproduction, flight or fight, and hunger were stimulated by chemicals from what we now call our mid-brain. For millions of years, the best these people could come up with was a flat stone or bone edge to scrape items for use, which demonstrates minimal development of the thinking part, technically called the neo-cortex. But let's not get hung up on lingo here.

Something happened in our history to propel humans into civilisation, which occurred historically, anthropologically, and biologically, almost overnight, if we consider how slow evolution is. Humans grew a bigger brain! Once humans inherited the enormous top area for thinking, complex ideas could be constructed and enacted in the real world. Outside of the exceedingly slow laws of evolution, according to questionable models of anthropology, about 30,000–50,000 years ago they began making ornaments, effigies, and jewellery, among many examples; then, even more extraordinarily, at roughly 10,000 years ago, written script, permanent housing, crops, and animal husbandry appeared. It is by these examples we use the term civilisation. Organisation, planning, and expansion are the result of the new improved layer: the *thinking* neo-cortex.

This then raises questions about the enduring purpose of emotions and hormones following this upgrade, and leaves us still wondering about the role of the lower part of the brain. Where is instinct's place in the evolved human now when there is an infinite library of ideas to draw from in everyone's brain? It is a good question. Recall earlier when I described that emotions come after a thought or event? This suggests, or affirms, that emotions are the after effect of the experience, which could be termed the evaluators, where we work to create something then we *feel* our accomplishments or failures. Conversely, we could also label the hormones that urge humans to eat or procreate, as the motivators. To explore the remaining lower part, called the cerebellum, then, I'll provide a couple of visuals that outline its purpose and function, garnered from a few documentaries I've seen. As you'll see, it doesn't think – it *knows* – and it's this part we access during determined focus.

The following two scenarios include the use of a mechanical arm experts use to remotely repair a fault in either humans or machinery. Firstly, onboard the International Space Station there is an external device for repairing damage to the outside, that is manoeuvred by people using hand sized controllers viewed on a monitor. Because they are not moving their own hands and fingers in a predictable fashion, the brain can only transfer the *intent* to the intermediary gears, that is again uniquely translated to the object of repair. One operator described how they can't *think* how to move the outside arm, because it's not attached to them, but instead they must maintain focus on the external piece, and just let their hands toggle the gear sticks *automatically*. Similarly, when doctors perform intricate keyhole surgery requiring tiny mechanical tools, they also describe watching the monitor and operating equipment *without* thinking. If these abilities are neither thought nor felt into action, then it leaves only the lower cerebellum responsible for *knowing*. Abstract, holistic, and unpremeditated in its function; the lower cerebellum is the perfect interface between humans and the divine.

Comparatively understanding the upper brain portion's functions to the lowest region gives us clarity in knowing why it is employed for disciplines. When we have something on our mind that we are constantly *thinking* about for possible solutions, or deciphering causal factors for its occurrence, we struggle to arrive at any finite conclusion. Such rumination also provokes unruly emotions that loop the issue over and over with little resolve. Then one day, when our mind is temporarily empty, we get a sudden realisation – a visual flash – that contains all the information. This unhindered portion is where we can practice moving to if we wish to shift from the primitive human to our Creator self.

This part of our brain is what Ram terms the mother/father principle – the overseeing original parent. Deliberately included in the human model, as it scaled and recorded millions of years of experience, it sat quietly there to be drawn on by the occupying spirit, when asked the bigger questions. The opportunity for enlightenment was ever ready, enduring and patient, as long as the noise was silenced long enough for an uninterrupted view by the cerebellum. From these simplified understandings, we can employ the parts of the brain for living *and* spiritual evolution, as opposed to just mindless existing. By first constructing what we want by design, we then engage in our endeavours to get the emotional feedback, good or bad, and the experience is thus known and added to the library of our individual Soul.

This leads us to further wonder about the breadth of information accessible, if every possibility is *known* in the cerebellum. In the bible, which I made a point of reading, because you can't argue against religion unless you know what you're talking about, it says in Ecclesiastes that "there is nothing new in the world". Interesting comment; and hardly a biblical quote worth remembering, which can be understood two ways. Firstly, that there is inheritance from eons of human experience passed through birth in the neurons to access, or secondly, that time and its linear quality – from past to future – may not be as fixed as we think.

If the latter were true, as I believe it is, then time is only relative to the three-dimensional world of height, depth, and width that we perceive. Travel from A to B takes time, so beings in UFOs traversing incredible distances – and I mean through a universe so expansive it boggles the mind – should have died millions of years before arriving. Unless: they direct their destination onto the craft *outside* of time, then drop back in when and where they desire, in a moment. If any possible place and time can be thought of, then these galaxy travellers must have all past and future information stored in their brains. To do so, the cerebellum – for all of us – must therefore be capable of operating outside the confines of fixed reality, and naturally it makes sense then, that there is nothing new in the world.

If we return to the idea of inheriting a larger neo-cortex in the brain, by exploring human evolution, the introduction of the new upper layer suggests there was outside intervention. When I taught ancient history over the years, I would show students the excessively long time it took for humans to evolve, by contrasting it with the sudden biological change to our brains, using a simple visual.

I would go to a corner of the classroom and suggest it was the start of the human species, using the walls as a timeline. I'd walk slowly from corner to corner, with my fingers tracing each wall as a million years, starting from the simplest primate, and describing how the best we could come up with was a stone tool. At the fourth wall, I would stop my finger a few centimetres from where I'd begun, and say this was the point of intellectual explosion from being stone-age nomads to living in cities, with complex writing, laws, dense living, agriculture, technology, and so forth. They'd aways just sit quietly and stare. Everyone was processing the expansive unchanging history to the sudden advancement of contemporary human beings and civilisation, coupled with the enlarged neo-cortex behind the forehead.

The demonstration showed that the change could not be subtle and evolutionary. I could never include for students my hypothesis that advanced races genetically introduced the increased brain capacity. It was okay for some science teachers to refuse to teach evolution in the grades it was taught, steadfastly sticking to the creation story of religion, but I could in no way discuss this possibility in my classes.

Ironically, I found a way of inferring external intervention using religion as my evidence, which planted interesting seeds of inquiry. I would refer to the genesis chapter of the Old Testament, where it says that in the beginning God created us in his likeness. I'd then explain the Hebrew word for God in the original text, Elohim, was plural. That was always discussion worthy. Next, I'd show the cylinder seal from ancient Iraq, that depicted a woman holding up a baby, and inform them that cuneiform text from this time described it as their creation story. Clearly a human, with other people present, it was not difficult to infer the original creator was a female, as you could easily see the breasts. I always suggested that theorising using evidence is at the discretion of those doing the interpretation, and was never fixed or final as long as new evidence was being uncovered.

Over the years, I'd read so many alternative historical texts that eventually I got better at drawing incredible links to push kid's thinking outside the box. If I was to brag about who was the best history teacher in my schools, I'd have to put my hand up! I could

Chapter 10: The Sonic Boom

have the most disruptive, poorly behaved kids in the school spellbound, and after a few lessons into the term, they'd say, "You're the only teacher I be good for", or "This is the only class I come on time to". So funny, but who could blame them? School is often bloody boring, and somewhere in their minds they know there is no logic for regular teaching material, like the standard pyramid theories tossed around. This truth must exist in the *knowing* brain, and we are just dumbing them down.

My best lessons were hypothesising the purpose of the pyramids, after establishing that there was no evidence of them being tombs. I would ask students to share possibilities for their purpose; and why they'd make them so incredibly durable as to not wither away into ruins, as other architectural feats in the world had. I also asked them to discuss why they were four sided triangular structures, and not right-angled oblong ones like the Athenian Acropolis, for example. Man, they were always hooked.

This is when I'd do my next visual representation with curious kids – every damned one of them, I might add. I'd ask them to draw a large see-through cube on their book or laptop. "Make it big", I'd say, "You're gonna need to draw inside it". Some kids struggled to do this, and as a guide I'd draw it on the whiteboard too. I would then ask them to look around the classroom and note it looked somewhat like the cube they drew. They all agreed it had the three dimensions of height, depth, and width.

I'd point at the top of one corner of the ceiling and ask them to place their pen or laptop mouse on the same spot of their diagram. Next, I would trace my finger through the air, downwards from this upper corner, through the centre of the room to the opposite bottom corner. I would then draw this diagonal line through my cube, as did they. They could use a different colour for distinguishing the cube lines from the inner diagonal lines if it helped. Then I would raise my finger to the next top corner of the ceiling and trace it through the centre of the classroom to the other opposite bottom corner. They, too, would locate this on their diagram to draw, usually copying mine on the board.

After the four diagonal lines from the visual display were copied to the drawn display, I would ask someone to point to the spot in the room where the diagonal lines all crossed. Someone nearby would place their pointed finger in the air where these lines all met, at centre of the classroom. Waiting for explanation, the kids never took their eyes off the spot. I'd remind them of the cube's dimensions of height, width, and depth, then ask them, "Is this spot either height, width or depth?". All of them would chorus, "No". I'd then ask, if this spot in the centre of the room was neither of those, what could we call this point? Swear to God, if you could hear cogs going in the brain it would've been an orchestra! I'd ask them if they could agree to this point being a *zero point*; after all it was neither of the three familiar dimensions. All the students, regardless of temperament, would sit spellbound with quiet anticipation, every single time.

Then, I'd ask them to choose another colour pen or computer shade, and instruct them to copy my colouring in. Within its diagonal lines only, starting from the centre of the cube, we'd all shade downward to the lower edge, where a pyramid shape becomes apparent.

You can't just leave the revelation of its design there – you have to be arriving at something. I'd introduce the idea that perhaps there may be a symbolic purpose to the lasting design these phenomenal engineers left behind. I wasn't going to spoon feed them too quickly, this would be plain old indoctrination, and as I've already said: we can't tell someone to believe something, it must be understood to sustain the knowledge. I would then ask them to nut out the purpose as to why this pyramid shape, as a symbol, may have been deliberately built to withstand time, as a legacy of sorts.

We had to explore what the shape might mean. After discussing that the lower part of the pyramid needed to be stronger to hold the weight, I'd prompt them to chew on ideas of the bottom half also being bigger to reflect the three dimensions it existed in. Then we'd explore why it was gradually reduced to a point that belonged to none of the dimensions, and the possible meaning therein. We'd have suggestions about what this symbolised to people, if we assume master engineers wanted an audience through the ages.

The teenagers mostly did not arrive at any conclusions about this, so I'd encourage them to wonder what other cultural or religious symbolism existed that may be similar in shape. Again, no surprises they never found any tangible similarities, so I'd introduce the most familiar object I'd garnered from Ram: the Christmas tree.

This is just the most magic demonstration of quantum physics worthy of elaboration, but to deliver it as I did in the classroom, I'll keep it simple. Shaped like a narrow pyramid, I'd draw a rough image on the whiteboard with a green marker. Next, I'd brainstorm what was usually atop the tree, with a "star or angel" eagerly called out. I always stuck with the star to have less religiosity, noting the star's five parts also resembled a head and limbs – a glittering representation of people, if you will. Drawing links between the treetop and the pyramid's point to reiterate the spot where the physical dimensions converged into nothing, I'd ask what else we decorated them with.

After excited callouts by kids, I'd describe the shining baubles as being representative of our imagination, and the descending spiral of tinsel being our ideas coalesced into physical gifts at its base. This always generated "aaahs" from the audience, even from the most motley crew. Superbly self-evident, this familiar image embodies the simple physics of collapsing matter from energy by observation from the shining mind at the top. With no intellectualism needed – its sublime knowledge belongs to everyone.

This would be when I'd bring up the picture of the blue Hindu god Shiva in a seated position. Ramtha has an extraordinary teaching and discipline on this image, so it wasn't my own genius coming up with that. The diagram shows a being with eyes closed or lowered, and legs crossed in a familiar meditative pose. I'd linearly trace on the whiteboard around the seated person to reveal the triangular shape. I'd note the sun placed behind the figure and the moon at its front, where the individual existed in the middle of two metaphorical worlds; those being: the obvious visual world at its rear, and the mysterious one at the fore, noting that its attention faced the latter.

I'd examine the props around the seated Shiva to deconstruct the symbolism; exploring the dead tiger it sat upon as the primal aspect of mankind, the pearls around the neck as the opalesced callouses of experience and wisdom, and the three-pronged trident as the slayer of the material, three-dimensional world. Finally, we'd brainstorm the different parts of the human body and their purposes. Likening the bottom half of the Shiva to the densest part of the pyramid, we could agree that the body's lower regions were crucial in the physical world for its survival. This included running for hunting or escaping, reproduction, and where the digestive tract rested. Then we'd note the upper, narrower half of the seated image, and how these areas ventured into less visible ideas of breathing, speaking, and thinking.

Next, they'd be instructed to research quickly on their laptops the meaning of the word pyramid. "Oooooh", they'd whisper, after finding out it meant 'fire in the middle' in Greek, after which they had to find out what was in the centre of the biggest structure. I'd then show them the innocuous image of the King's chamber, where no hieroglyphs were present, an unadorned lone stone sarcophagi sat, and granite slabs laid precisely one above the other over the chamber. Everyone could agree this could be considered the heart of the pyramid.

We would then draw links between the King's chamber and the Shiva image. I'd draw lines between the head, chest, and abdomen, to show three parts, highlighting the chest as its own 'fire in the middle'; essentially making this as the crossing point from the physical to the invisible aspects of the human already discussed.

Referring to our original purpose, of hypothesising the great pyramid's enduring meaning, awesome conversations always ensued. When paired to other images and their symbolism, the material world descending from the immaterial becomes unmissable.

Chapter 10: The Sonic Boom

And to the rest of the world: they are just a burial chamber.

I seemed to have also acquired the behaviour of teaching people in my regular life. It's no wonder over the years I've heard people complain about teachers being know-alls, as I think we get used to telling people things we've learnt, or troubleshooting and helping people find ways to improve things. I was always motivated to change my ex-husband, hoping he'd fit my program in front of my parents and friends, so they'd never see who he really was, instead of admitting I'd fucked up. Trying to save face, as they call it, was like trying to squeeze a square through a circle for the thirteen years I held it together.

I was always attempting to imprint on him my spiritual understandings under the guise of getting somewhere or succeeding in life. Such bullshit. I was really trying to stage a façade of him being a good person and get him to earn more money, although I didn't acknowledge this at the time.

My mum was temporarily living with us at one stage when she caught him sorting through prostitutes on his phone, saving his preferred ones. When confronted in front of us three girls, he yelled at her to get out of his house for lying. I felt so sorry for her, but I said nothing in her defence because I was afraid of him. She had nowhere to go; and biting her tongue, stayed largely isolated in her room until she could leave a few months later.

I had experienced him doing this myself some time before. Early one morning, as he chain-smoked outside, I crept up to look through the window behind him. I nearly fainted at the realisation of what he was doing. Now he was exposing his true self to my parent, and I was terrified of it coming out to everyone. My brother and I had also had a falling out from the beginning over the "tea towel head", and now I was at risk of having my whole family turn from me.

One night, I was again trying to gently persuade him to think and act like me. It was in his best interests to pay attention, as he relied on my income for sending $500US a month to his mum in Egypt. I spoke long and measuredly in the dark hours about the purpose of life, spiritually speaking, and was attempting to reach him by elaborating on the concepts I've shared here.

Without warning, a thunderous boom occurred. The entire house shook, reverberating the glass in every window from the force. The explosion couldn't be isolated as occurring above or below us, as the sound and movement were felt in all directions. I haven't experienced a bomb going off, but from what I'd seen in films where a building is blown up, it had the same intensity. I immediately thought the sewer pipes under the house had caught fire from methane or something, and we ran quickly to the balcony to decipher what was the cause.

From such a huge noise, we expected the neighbour's dogs to be barking hysterically, as they did when teens set off firecrackers in the park nearby. Instead, it was dead quiet. And I mean eery, total silence. There was no way that huge sound had not startled any animal, and we could not hear any of our neighbours abruptly open their windows and sliding doors to investigate. No one had heard it. How could the tremendous sound have been isolated to our house alone?

Then I remembered something from planes that travelled faster than the speed of sound: sonic booms. I'd seen this on TV. This was exactly what I'd heard. There was no plane to see, and we would have heard its engines on its trajectory before and after, which there were none, and this sound would've rattled the neighbouring dogs also. There was no movement in the trees – dead still. It was definitely a sonic boom, but I couldn't attribute it to UFOs either. I'd seen them take off from a standstill at supersonic speeds, and they didn't have a dot of sound.

If it was a UFO listening to me preach on, they were probably endeavouring to shut me up. He was feigning listening, and it wasn't

Chapter 10: The Sonic Boom

my duty to persuade him anyway. Rather than give in to the truth that I'd married a lazy, porn addicted man, I remained determined to paddling up shit creek for the next five years. Not only that: I ended up in a barbed wire canoe with no paddle.

When he went to visit his mum in 2010, she gave him twenty grand as an advanced inheritance. I was so pissed. Throughout the preceding years with him I had returned to full-time work with a newborn, taken on international students at his insistence, whom I had to run around, wash, shop and cook for, so he could send her money. A bloody fortune to us at the time, but I couldn't bear the thought of her going hungry, so forfeited niceties and quality time with my daughters to look after her. Like me, he put on a show to pretend how well he'd done for himself moving to a foreign country.

Around this time, he fell asleep at the wheel driving home one shift. A brand-new car, still owing thirteen grand to the bank, was a total write off. I'd not renewed the insurance a couple of months before because money was so scant, and he'd had seven or eight other accidents in the years prior that I forked out endless money for. One two-week period he accrued four traffic infringement tickets for speeding, and so excessively that each were over $800. I put it down to being overwhelmed by his mum's cancer news, and assumed he wasn't sleeping well during the day while I worked.

I'd arranged a term off school at the time, to be a proper mum to my little girl for three months, when he returned without the money. He'd spent it all on Arabic furniture, envisioning himself as an importing baron. I arranged a warehouse at great expense, where the stuff went upon his return, but it just sat there. And it sat there some more. Livid at the situation, I decided I was going to get every penny back, so killed myself selling it online and lost the entire three months working from 4am to 8pm, seven days a week.

And, taking a strap to my back by not stopping there, I took working harder to a whole new level after returning to teaching.

CHAPTER ELEVEN

The Constellation

Around this period, I had a long-time dream fulfilled of buying a picturesque acreage of land in the mountains. It was located behind where we'd newly moved to, after finally leaving numb nuts behind. Four acres of beauty resembling an English countryside, but I then needed money for two mortgages, and discovered land this size does not stay pristine for free.

I gave myself a one-year deadline to sell the junk furniture. He'd been so arrogant, that when he walked around showrooms in Cairo asking for this and that, like a celebrity on an antique splurge, he had not checked any of it. The stock was old, broken, and stained – obviously the crap they wanted to get rid of. To fix it before leaving for work at 7am, and dropping both girls in different directions, I had to start getting up at three in the morning to do my disciplines. I wasn't going to let them slide as I wanted to manifest money without having all the hard work. To give up labour, however, would mean giving up being a martyr – so that didn't happen. Nonetheless, I applied myself in my ignorance all the same.

My routine always started with coffee of course, followed by a walking discipline Ram calls the Neighbourhood Walk®, named for its premise in getting us out of old paradigms of thoughts and into

Chapter 11: The Constellation

new areas unused by the brain. Then, sitting quietly after my brain was on fire, I'd do the grid. I always sat at the rear of my house by the large sliding glass door, gazing up at the starry sky. I wasn't actually looking at the sky, remember, but staring a few metres in the air in front of me. Sometimes I could visibly see patches of the grid fading in and out of the area I was focussed on. This usually means I'm doing the discipline correctly, at least that's what I infer.

On one occasion, I drifted out of focus and found myself staring at a constellation. The stars are always beautiful, and not overly preventative to getting back into focus. As I gazed fondly at this formation of about five or six stars, the whole constellation began to gently move and disseminate. Again, right in the centre of my gaze! They drifted to my right, and some moved ahead of the others, spreading apart a little. Holy shit: it wasn't a constellation at all, it was a squadron of UFOs! 'Wow!', I thought elatedly. 'A whole bloody fleet'. I watched them drift off out of sight for a minute or so, happy that it had occurred on my watch.

At the risk of sounding repetitive, I again wondered what part of this was my doing, if at all, and for what purpose. I can't imagine that inter-stellar vehicles with intelligent beings would drop what they were doing, announce that a human was practicing quantum magic, and quickly get over here to watch. Remembering their little visits were brief – they were hardly worth pausing in between their universal business to say "Hi" for. Perhaps they were already stationed around the Earth, overlooking their creation in a familial, endearing way, and observing how primitive humans were utilising their genetic inheritance.

ETs overseeing the human race, according to Ramtha and other corroborative sources, met with President Eisenhower in the '50s, to give him an interesting gift. Called the Yellow Box, it was a device that showed the future to whomever peered into it. International dignitaries in the know flew in to have a look, so to speak, much to their horror when they did. Each of the different times they looked at it they saw varying outcomes. Their actions and intent in between views was altering the course slightly, and this frightened them. In most instances they saw their own demise, with their power and control wiped away beforehand. Like cave men arguing over a new tool offered by the Gods, they failed to see its purpose. The ETs had intended for it to make them aware of their consciousness and the changeability of it on their future. Shaking their heads at their behaviours, the visitors allegedly retrieved the device from them.

Looking back, I used to narrow my understanding of UFOs present during my focus as a side effect of the discipline. I couldn't think outside of my own box of perception, much like I'd highlighted about archaeologist's coming to their own small conclusions. Retrospectively, however, an idea around timelines and futures later emerged.

During the period of having my new home and acreage, I stumbled on the second book I was compelled to have: *The Lost Book of Enki*, by Zecharia Sitchin. I never read books twice, as I barely had time to, but this one was the exception. I can't quite put my finger on it, but it feels more familiar to me than I can convey. In the text, which is a translation of Sumerian cuneiform, it depicts a genesis project on Earth.

It cites more than one occasion where humans were created by beings three billion years ahead in evolution than our own. That affords an extraordinary advancement ahead of ours, and one can only imagine where they're at intellectually and spiritually. They used their own eggs for integrating with early hominids here, tweaking the DNA until it resembled their own, but with some distinguishable features to differentiate us from them. I'm certain this is when and why the sudden evolution in human beings took place, altering our neocortex to facilitate creative ideas for forming civilisations

Chapter 11: The Constellation

here. What a gift to give us such a huge nudge forward. Accordingly, they have curiously observed our progress for millennia.

I wondered over the years whether our new additions to the brain may be in conflict with our primitive instinctual operations, that relied on hormones and emotions. The relatively short time between the earlier brain to the new upgrade may have created a house divided against itself that needs nutting out, either via the long haul of time and experience, or by advanced guidance.

If we have an animal-like body, relying on senses and hormones to trigger us into action, this could issue tendencies that override a brain trying to construct new possibilities. This is perhaps a reason why humans have trouble deciding on things and give in to situations against our better interests. We recognise subtly that we're letting feelings guide us, while we ignore fleeting glimpses of insight that offer more optimal courses of action. This distinction, or conflict rather, may be why we attempt to resolve problems deciphering between our head and our heart, as they say. The problem with this phrase is no one knows which one they're meant to listen to! I think I've distinguished this for us to know better.

One night during my 3am focus, something alerted my eyes upward. It was the gold disk again, exactly the same one above my car decades before. Beautiful, gold light emanated homogenously all over the base, which meant I couldn't see the material it was made of, nor any discernible light sources therein. They had come back. I wonder how many times it might have done so that I hadn't seen, caught up in my life's dramas? My house is two story, and the disk emerged overhead from the roof. There are trees about five metres in front of that, so I only had the few seconds it glided out and over me. As its height was roughly six or seven metres off the ground, it appeared to be about two metres wide.

For some strange reason I never contemplated the occupants on this occasion. Now, though, I think they may have been absolutely tiny! That, or no one was even in it. Perhaps it was remotely controlled, or it could be something quite different altogether, judging by their technological advancement.

Some months ago, I had a spontaneous flash of information, or *knowingness*, relevant to the sizes of some of the craft. I was doing focus when my mind went to the abstract idea that these vehicles, which are created to transcend time and spatial dimensions, may appear small to us from our perspective, but not necessarily so from theirs. Like Einstein's relativity theory, or his wife's, rather, if you've heard about her own genius: if we are in a different speed of time or frequency, it feels normal when we're in it. This suggests, relative to their experience, the beings may be comfortably sitting in their actual size, within a bigger ship, and perceived as smaller in our world. Food for thought anyway, and one day I expect to find out.

It was during this period that I also had an unusual experience – or encounter, which is perhaps a better word to describe it. I often waited for my husband to fall asleep to do a particular focus in the dark, sitting up in bed with blindfolds on. I remember I was practicing experiencing the black Void, from whence we all come, and remain connected to. I wanted to be familiar with it, to know its non-spatial, non-linear qualities. After a period, I would have a sense of no longer being in a body, which is the best way I can explain it.

On one occasion, an almost typical looking alien appeared in this alternate state – very real and vivid. It was close enough to almost touch my face with its own, such that I instantly recoiled. It wasn't grey as I would have expected, but cream coloured; and although I only had the opportunity to note its face and neck, I could sense it was much taller, and narrower in its head than I'd seen in the media. It had the up-turned, solid black eyes, with flawlessly smooth skin, but it looked more inter-dimensional in quality rather than physical, if that makes sense.

It scared me, but not because it had frightening features or some nebulous aura of evil about it. My response was the unexpectedness of it, its proximity, and the contrast to my brain's paradigms about what living beings should look like. I hadn't been contemplating anything of this kind, and was in fact lost in a trance state, so the event was not contrived by my imagination. The spontaneous apparition was a test of my approachability, and I clearly failed in my readiness for conscious contact.

CHAPTER TWELVE

The Shooting Star

I went to work at a new high school in 2012, closer to the present home, as my other school had hired a tyrant of a principal. In fact, three of us moved from there to the new school, as everyone became frightened from Code of Conduct investigations being issued to some staff for seemingly inconsequential things. It was excellent at the new school for a while, as they valued me, and this gave me some provisional self-worth. Like all things garnered from us externally – they never last.

I was working long hours at this school also, but I was happy to because they praised my rapport with the difficult kids, and quite honestly, I was used to it. Every Sunday I would also go by myself to the land and work for five or six hours. Sustaining this meant valuable time was spent away from my girls, especially my littlie, who'd largely grown up without me.

Instead of it being a healing experience, pottering around my hidden idyll, I was always absorbed by hatred for my life. All the cockups I'd faced, like the enduring cover-up of my marriage, my husband's blowing of thousands of dollars on useless shit, and his supreme laziness, would be stewed over and over in my head. I was perpetuating my suffering in my body, and onto the quantum field

Chapter 12: The Shooting Star

for my future. The more I held my focus on misery, the more I got. That's the law of freewill and manifesting. If only I'd had the maturity to know that I could have focused on happier, better times to manifest as smoothly as I did suffering.

The maintenance of the grass was a drain on financial resources, but it had to be done. The first time I had it razed, there was a dead brown snake chopped up from the blades. It had the thickness of my forearm, and although it was dead, I was paralysed by fear just looking at it. I wandered only a couple of metres from that frightful mess to find myself facing a live, red-bellied black snake, with head elevated and erect, staring at me. I nearly fainted. When I say I was shaking, and both my arms were weak for two hours – I am not exaggerating!

My solution would be to acquire two cows. I located a breeder of Scottish Highlanders nearby, quite fortuitously it seems, for another curious reason. When I drove up to the property, located literally thousands of feet above sea level, my daughter and I spotted an alien street sign on the fence. It had the usual 'grey' shaped head and recognisable black eyes, with "Aliens come here", or something to that effect written on it. "Is he taking the piss you reckon?", I asked my eldest daughter. We weren't sure, but it was proving interesting beyond just buying cattle.

The man took us up to a huge enclosure that overlooked the entire Gold Coast, with dozens of calves and giant beasts to choose from. They are the most stunning animals you can imagine, but I expressed concern about the thickness of the coat in a hot climate. I then asked him about the sign on the fence.

Bugger me. He had more than an interest in UFOs, he was trained by Dr Steven Greer in using consciousness for ET contact, when leading groups. He showed us images of Dr Greer present on his property, initiating people on the protocols, and had otherworldly pictures of interesting phenomena they'd caught in the process. There were unusual streams of light caught among the group using infra-red cameras, and other anomalies, as the term goes when describing inclusions that can't be explained. I elaborated on some of my own experiences, and he invited us up for an evening to test my own techniques. He agreed to let my daughter and I do our thing, and he would bring his camera and green laser light.

The night arrived with a torrential downpour. I didn't want to reschedule because I normally had zero disposable time, so kept our original appointment. Up on the mountain we could barely open our eyes from the pelting rain. I had no idea that being so high up would also include a drop in about ten degrees, and we absolutely froze. I even had to sit in between the man's legs with his jacket over me, quite uncomfortably since I didn't know him, and there were predictably no results. Had it been a clear night it would have been incredibly beautiful with the clear vista of the coastal city, even if there were no UFOs to be had. There were also glow worms lining the road to our car, which greatly enhanced the magic of this location.

I bought two steers, quite inexpensively, and named them William and Wallace. The little boys would fare well in their elevated new home with their shaggy coats, as I had a tiny forest for them to shade under, and a spring fed pond to bath or drink from; and it didn't take long for those mower mouths to clean up my property and grow into Minotaurs in the process. It was also soon obvious they'd been missed in the castration process, and it made the neighbours and I nervous at the prospect of having two frisky bulls kept in by the flimsy wire fencing.

During this period, my husband bought a new Smartphone that ultimately opened a Pandora's box to the extent of his secret behaviours. I often pressed the screen button during the night, for a bit of light to use the toilet or start my focus, but usually received a bit more than light. I can't say how many times there'd be a message from an undisclosed number, with texts such as "Hey babe, how far away are

Chapter 12: The Shooting Star

you?" or "I look forward to pleasuring you". I'd record the number from his phone and search it online later. It was mostly prostitutes, and others had no results. Didn't matter – they were evidently about having sex. These things would destroy me in the following years.

He was working as a waiter by this time, so when he woke up, I'd question it. Lies, lies and more lies, certainly, but his excuses would always win me over somehow. Probably because it would often escalate to him punching me, bruising my arms and chest, or throwing me into a wall or up the stairs if I was trying to leave. What was I to do? It'd shatter my family and I'd lose my land. Let me reiterate: I'd had enough understanding and proof of our abilities to create something better, but when we're sucked into an emotional barrage, it's almost impossible to move into the areas of the brain that focus requires. Exhaustion too – I had more than any human being could bear.

There were many instances of these texts occurring, and other strange things he had to make up stories for, that it – or I – was becoming a joke. I made the unethical decision to hack into his email to know more. It took about two attempts, and it was our wedding date. Once in, I found years of emails arranging for women to come to our house for sex while I was at work, and numerous sex groups he was a member of. I could even open the profiles and read his write ups and see the pictures I'd taken of him. You can imagine the blood running out of my face at this discovery, and the disappointment at the disregard for all my self-sacrificing of time and money.

I could see the dates spanning difficult periods, including during the three years of torment from the neighbour. He'd obviously never cared. No wonder he fell asleep at the wheel: he was up all night with his head in muck and getting his end in by day – the whole bloody time. I tried desperately to get rid of him, but he would just laugh arrogantly at me and say he wasn't leaving his home. If I stayed adamant, he would wear me out, harassing me for nights and weeks on end till I was broken. You can only go to school on no sleep for so long, with a fake cheer and smile, till you're absolutely fucked.

One day, a neighbour next to my land phoned to say my two giants had gotten out of the fencing and were wandering the streets. I'd discovered another sex text in the early hours, but I had to swallow my pride and bring him with me to chase the bulls several kilometres back to my land. Once found, we had to perilously chase the buggers amid oncoming cars. All I could think of was an unwitting car turning a bend and slamming into one of them. They were enormous, with horns that'd rip through a windscreen and impale the driver. I was absolutely terrified I'd be sued to eternity, with the added burden of dealing with an adulterous asshole at the same time. Something had to give.

Unfortunately, it would be my 'Bravehearts' first. I noticed one day that the white bull, William, was covered in grape-sized green balls – possibly hundreds – and I had no idea what they were. A neighbour rang to say he was laying down struggling to breathe, but by the time I arrived he was dead. Paralysis ticks. I had him buried for a small fortune on the land, and someone – or some group of collaborators – decided the other had to go too.

I arrived for my regular day on the land to find Wallace missing. The immediate neighbour said he'd jumped the fence facing the dairy, that occupied the valley to the north side. This fence wasn't my clumsy installation, but the farmer's legitimate steel one for his business. There was as much chance of that beast successfully jumping that fence as there was me scaling from a single bound. No way in hell did he jump. I knew the sight of his huge hung balls terrified residents around us, especially with a herd of enticing heifers on the other side. I guess it was the right thing to do. I hope whoever got him enjoyed his meat at least; it would have fed a family for a year.

In the interim, I had already paid for a concrete cabin to be put on the property. I wanted it buried with only the side open that faced away from the road, overlooking the picturesque valley. The builders had offered an engineer certified one, and knew I wasn't declaring it for council approval. Taking advantage of my elusive requests, a

Chapter 12: The Shooting Star

dud was delivered. No certificate of safety, and light peered through all the concrete blocks thrown together. It was too risky to enter, even without soil on top, and they blew me off at every phone call. I'd forked out seventeen grand, after also having the hole dug and a crane hired to place it.

I decided I'd had a gutful of people taking the piss, so applied to take them to court. Being a teacher, I dredged up every piece of correspondence, had it meticulously arranged and entered as evidence, to represent myself. Of the three court appearances, where I waited in the foyer sitting across from them shaking and breathless, the first obviously proved to be the worst.

As all of us sat before the magistrate, the court attendant came over with the bible for me to swear to tell the truth. Uncompromising, I said I wouldn't swear on the bible because I'm not religious, so he gave me something else to read. The two dudes, dressed in their borrowed suits, were also not experienced in swearing under these circumstances. They'd clearly watched too much TV court dramas, and automatically tagged on the end of their oaths, "So help me god". I had an inner giggle, which put me at ease, as the script didn't include this bit, but doing their darndest to impress the audience they went Hollywood in their attempt.

I didn't realise winning just means you win. They don't necessarily have to pay, and that requires an enforcement order, and another court appearance if you want your money. I couldn't bear any more court appearances and sent notice that I'd attend via phone. As events were unfolding, I remembered the notion of tangible evidence needed in the justice system, after dealing with my mad neighbour, and I had an opportunity to get a bit of my own back. Quite unlike me, and surprising even to myself, I had a moment of go-fuck-yourself towards the builders from all my dilemmas.

The bailiff, at least that's what I think he was, said the men agreed to returning ten thousand on condition that I let them retrieve the cabin. It was useless to me in its perilous condition, but it may have been restored. I agreed; and he instructed me immediately to put my approval in writing via email as soon as I saw the dollars deposited in my bank. I can't recall how long it took, but as soon as I spotted my money, heart pounding right up to my neck, I emailed the magistrate. Instead of simply accepting the agreed amount, I included that upon them fulfilling the remainder up to $17,000 then they could come and collect it. Boom! Within minutes the bailiff was screaming how he'd have me arrested, among other things, and how I'd embarrassed him in court. Among many of my spontaneous comments, one was "go ahead, I've put the agreement in writing". I'd never been this bold in my life, and I waited in terror. Nothing. I was genuinely sorry to have humiliated him, but I wasn't sorry enough to care above my own problems in that moment.

I knew I was only tolerating my husband's lies to keep my land. I'd decided some months before, after so many cheating incidences, that I'd use him for his meagre income. When I think about it now, I had always used him. Mutual usury – my income for prostitutes, and his money for presenting a fake success story to everyone.

I never spent my nights relaxing during this period. As any parent does, I'd come home and cook, clean, and pick up after everyone. If I had some free minutes, I'd sit outside for a quick grid session. I knew the grid worked; I'd proven it time and again, even if I wasn't awake to what it could truly be used for, and it was easy to do when you're knackered.

Sitting outside for a spell one night, I began doing the discipline. I could hear the TV going inside, and periodically my youngest girl, then aged four, would pop out to ask me something. I'd only focussed for about ten minutes when she stood next to me talking. With my head facing her, she suddenly stopped and pointed to my right, saying, "Look mum, a shooting star!". Let me just say – there was no shooting star. I turned immediately to find a fully formed

Chapter 12: The Shooting Star

UFO in gloriously lit splendour only metres from us. I could never compare any of them present with me – every single one was a wonder beyond any expectation. But the details of this craft were the pièce de resistance.

Extending the anticipation for a minute, I have to say that her calling it a shooting star has always puzzled me. Obviously, she knew what a shooting star was to call it out, but this dynamo's dimensions were as high as a van and wide as a mini-bus, stationary, and right next to us! There could be no confusing this one.

The shape was surprisingly stereotypical in contrast to the ones my eldest daughter and I had had before. The craft was circular, and completely flat at its base, with no visible parts jutting out underneath. It had another smaller circular portion placed above its centre, with straight vertical sides, about a metre in height on its own, also flat on the top. I guess you'd say it looked like an upside-down noodle bowl.

Inside the 'standing room only' upper centrepiece there were three round portholes, completely black, and nothing visible therein. The bedroom light streamed towards it, yet there was obviously some technology stopping it from illuminating anyone inside. I could not see glass on the portholes that might reflect light, only dense blackness. The lower section, the largest and broadest part of the craft, was completely absent of any apparatus to depict parts or lights.

This UFO did not need lights.

Here's the most extraordinary part – and I hope I do it justice – the entirety of the craft's surface was not solid. It was condensed gold light. Not transparent either. Beyond words to describe, really. And it remained there long enough for me to absorb its every stunning detail.

Unlike the diamond, where I'd remotely given permission to take me up, I just sat in awe. I tried to look through the portholes – I wanted to see who was in there watching us. To this day, I cannot understand why I didn't go over to it. It was there longer than the others had been, and I could have walked over, waved, touched it, or called out. Why didn't I do this?! After a while, it floated ever so slowly across the small trees a few metres from me, and I could have passed through them and followed it. I wish I'd had the foresight to think this, but I imagine it's because one is just too stunned.

For years I pondered the shooting star term she'd used. Then one day it came to me. It must've shot down in a gold stream so fast that by the time she could verbalise this, it was there and present. Incredible.

I wonder now, if the craft was not solid, then perhaps the occupants may not be either, unless of course they have the technology to repel their feet from the base they stood on. Alternatively, they could possibly be inter-dimensional, and occupy physical bodies here at will if they so choose; given the unique technology displayed, anything is possible! This would be distinct from full-blown masters, however, who can manifest their bodies instantly with no craft. So much to contemplate. I also think about this craft having windows. All the other craft had none, and yet I knew they were sitting nearby because they could see me. This beauty certainly didn't need windows per se, but perhaps this is just a design choice. It could be that simple!

I can vividly recall the moment I decided that substituting my personal freedom to keep a man who was never going to love me, was a sell out to myself. Gardening in my present home, I knew I had to model strong womanhood in front of my daughters, and he had to go. Interestingly, my gold wedding ring fell off and was lost among the weeds somewhere, perfectly mirroring my decision. I concluded I had to sell my land and wait till the next time my husband was caught, to kick the prick out. I'd become so humiliated in front of my eldest daughter, by now doing her master's degree, and I couldn't bear that she looked on me pathetically for remaining with someone

Chapter 12: The Shooting Star

like him. I'd raised her to be greater, and I'd preached spiritual enlightenment all her life. What a fake I was, and a hypocrite too.

No surprises that I sold my pristine paradise quickly, where I made about sixty thousand dollars. Not much compared to the successes of my brother and dad, but a decent first for me. My husband thought it was his windfall, and he quit his job against my objections "to have a break". Very quickly I spotted a text flash when his phone sat unattended near me, and another a few hours later. It was on.

I don't need to elaborate much about the details, as the gaps can easily be filled by the imagination, but it did comprise of two arrests and six months of absolute torment. Like Mr Blood, after each arrest he was always back at our house. One night while I was cooking, and my youngest daughter was playing in her room upstairs, he appeared without invitation. I didn't hear him creep in, and suddenly felt him standing behind me. I acted calm, and continued to stir my food, when he put one arm around my neck and held me against his front, in a sort of mock headlock. I pretended I thought it was a type of hug and asked if he wanted any dinner. Slowly he turned me towards him, and held both hands around my throat. "You don't think I have the guts to do it, do you?", he said calmly.

On occasions in the past, when I chastised him about sleeping with strangers, I asked what he'd do if I had done it. He'd always laugh smugly and say I'd be buried in a hole somewhere. I can emphatically say that I believed in that moment this was my last night on earth. I managed to talk casually, distracting him long enough to step back, where I could grab my phone and run outside. Without alerting my youngest of any commotion, I persuaded him to go before I called the police. On this occasion, and many after, I decided I would not call them for breaching his domestic violence order. I knew if I did, a jail sentence would resolve him to planning my murder upon release.

CHAPTER THIRTEEN

The Wobble

Over the months of this period leading to Christmas 2015, I never took a single day off work. It was my bread and butter, and I was aspiring for leadership in the school. I could never let on to my colleagues or bosses that I had anything that may interfere with my performance. After losing nearly a quarter of a million in the divorce, I set my mind on becoming a Head of Department in my school. By the end of 2017 I'd become the co-ordinator for university graduates, or beginning teachers as we call them, and by 2018 I had thirteen staff I'd upskilled during their first year. I was so proud and rewarded by their overall success, but in all honesty, it was mostly for commendations from those that mattered.

Parallel to this, a former deputy from my old school ended up becoming our new principal, and I suspect he didn't like having staff from his past now present on his new appointment. We knew things about him that could have compromised his career, and he may have wondered if we did too. He also brought with him a cutthroat approach he'd acquired under the dictator we left behind, and things weren't looking good for anyone in the school.

It wasn't just that he increased our workload with infinite ideas he wanted implemented, the department also demanded more. I also

Chapter 13: The Wobble

noticed that the Queensland government was concurrently rebranding itself. We'd been the Sunshine State for decades, and this had a laid-back feel to it that they wanted to dismiss. Cars started having number plates labelled Smart State instead of the former; and instead of improving the quality of education cleverly for their new image, they simply quadrupled the workload. Time for marking and preparation hadn't been revised since I started in the nineties, and this caused absolute chaos for staff.

Choosing to increase my wage the difficult way, I said yes to anything my bosses asked of me. After all, I wanted something out of them, and deduced saying no would've made me look incompetent. Taking advantage of the need to fill my resume, the lazy oligarchs didn't hesitate to lob all their obligations onto me; and having little else in my cache to find self-worth, I nobly convinced myself to push on.

By now I was leaving for school by 6:45am and returning 5:30pm. I was expected to design from scratch a new curriculum program for the last two years of work-ready English, as I'd been the subject co-ordinator for years already. I still had a nearly full load of teaching senior classes, including university entrance subjects, on top of teaching beginning teachers how to do their job. As I was aspiring for leadership, I was also advised to host additional staff professional developments that needed hours of design and planning.

The principal also decided to change the school day from four periods a day to five. This seemingly tiny change was catastrophic for us, as we had to construct five lessons a day instead of four, and kids struggled having to focus on a fifth. I recall going to one Deputy and telling him I could never get my work done, as he'd been mentoring me for promotion, and I trusted his input. The principal came in, and I decided to tell him conversations staff were having about their difficulties coping with the increased number of periods.

He'd originally had to garner approval from staff on the change and ran a survey to make a democratic vote. My position teaching new staff meant I had to circulate among the staffrooms, where it became obvious to me that no one voted for an increase. Predictably, the results were never shown from the online survey, and no one dared ask to see them when it was announced that staff had overwhelmingly agreed.

Teachers were openly disclosing they were living off alcohol, enormous amounts in some cases, and others were increasing their antidepressants to cope with anxiety. Like other teachers, I would literally walk straight to the kitchen on my arrival home and skull wine from the bottle to come down. I usually couldn't get to sleep either, and would keep a bottle next to my bed to use like a sleeping pill. I couldn't go to school by seven o'clock on three hours of sleep, so it was just for survival.

Politely elaborating on staff discontent, I informed him how teachers were managing stress using substances. I thought he may have appreciated the honest discussion, but instead, this was perhaps the beginning of his dislike for me. I had inadvertently revealed the survey results were not as he claimed, and may have been on to his deception.

The extensive hours and work caused such terrible headaches that I'd be chugging down codeine and paracetamol by the truckload, including Valium from time to time. I was losing it, and again, something had to give. I'd pushed myself so hard, and felt I was too close to pack it in by then, so sacrificed my disciplines to get some extra sleep instead.

By the end of 2017 I had something strange occurring in my body. My left arm and leg began going numb. I'd have a tingle up the left side of my back also. I was so frightened I was getting Multiple Sclerosis or Motor Neuron's Disease that I went to different doctors on several occasions. None of them could definitively say what it was, and the fear compounded my symptoms.

Upon return to school in 2018, I remember almost passing out from terror during a three-hour staff meeting, believing I was going to fall down the two flights of stairs at its conclusion. I couldn't feel my left limbs, could barely move my leg or arm, and the skin on them burned cold. On the Friday afternoon I took myself off to emergency at the hospital, as I wanted immediate answers. The doctors arrived at it being anxiety. I thought this was an odd diagnosis for the symptoms, but I went on antidepressants anyway, and notified all the relevant bosses that I was taking medication. It suppressed the numb symptoms for a bit, except the headaches, and sensation of contraction of the skin on my face, so I kept up the drinking after hours to try to alleviate the symptoms.

With an excellent resume of staff leadership and curriculum design by now, I went for two promotional positions in the school, and to my surprise, I wasn't given an interview for either. This was against departmental protocols, and all the school staff knew what had occurred. It did wonders for my victim status, and my self-sacrificing martyr trip filled the gap on my lost self-worth. The second promotion was given to one of the beginning teachers I'd trained a couple of years before. Practically a kid, he became one of my bosses.

Something wasn't right.

I knew my principal had a hand in it. I suspect he didn't like that I wasn't a sycophant to him, as others were, or I'd continue to be objectionable to his endless remodelling of school processes. He was also regularly asking me for dirt on teachers, and even on my immediate Heads of Department (HOD), so when I wouldn't be his bitch, I guess it essentially marked the demise of my leadership aspirations.

Not giving up, I picked up my flagellant again, after advice from a different deputy to take on the additional role of Dean, managing welfare and behaviour for nearly four hundred kids. On top of this, I had to continue the curriculum design, and had double the teaching load than the other Deans, who weren't course writing. I didn't know then that this devastating load was setting me up to fail, and covertly pushing me out: I was too singular in my misused focus to see.

'Onward and upward', I thought, flagrantly tossing out my spiritual enlightenment and any mystical experiences that came with it. "It was only a bit further", I kept telling myself.

I spent the next two years nearly dying. I was often nearly passing out in classes, laying on the cold tiles of the disabled toilet floor to stop sweating from panic, and sobbing on the carpet of my office. Schoolwide, enough staff knew. I'd implored so many bosses by email that I wasn't coping, and on one occasion I primal cried in front of a class till I scared them. And kids talk. No one intervened on my behalf, and most recipients of my emails never replied. They knew what would happen if they did. They changed their tune suddenly, when I told one boss my arm was again numb from stress. By the end of the week, I was shipped out on sick leave.

My pride was hurt such that I impulsively enrolled in fulltime university. I was going to get my master's degree in youth counselling and come back blazing – on a higher wage than my HODs, and outrank them too. I was also embarrassed to tell my dad I'd failed – so I wanted to redeem myself to him. I studied and researched like a maniac, increasing antidepressants, and using migraine preventatives up to the eyeballs. I wasn't going to just qualify – I was going to have my degree with a distinction.

The subject matter was triggering me intensely, and I began to realise I couldn't go back to working in crisis situations with my own issues. The course materials revealed that my own experience in childhood had interfered with my cognitive processes through to now. I learnt definitively that children growing up in constant fear and yelling do not properly develop their executive function in the brain, the decision-making area. They dissociate from reality regularly when they can't escape situations in the home, and the flight or fight response turns off other cognitive operations one would normally acquire, had they the space and peace to develop them. As a

Chapter 13: The Wobble

result, kids in these circumstances become impulsive, and are also inclined to dismiss dangerous red flags in people that become their partners. This was me all over.

My eldest and I had some lovely quiet nights on my balcony after my husband no longer resided there. She'd literally spent his last few years hiding in her room to avoid him, and we were having some awesome chats in the dark. We'd spot satellites regularly, but on one occasion we had the feeling we were watching something quite different.

A very bright star was floating our way. We'd sat outside often enough over the years to identify planes, and could hear them and see their flashing lights to know anyway. There's a sense of height too, that you recognise where planes, helicopters and satellites are always placed. This star was abnormally luminous, like the planet Venus, but quite low in altitude and below where planes flew.

As it got closer, we both noticed and commented on its undeniable wobble. We'd never seen a wobbly plane or helicopter before, much less a totally bright one, and there was no sound associated with it. We both commented that it had to be a UFO, just as it passed over us. It wasn't close like other craft I've described, but it was close enough that we thought it should've been audible if it was an aircraft. We ran with my youngest girl in tow out the front to continue watching it sail by. I said, "Let's send it a message. Let's put a blue star inside the craft to show we're watching!". The blue star has a beautiful meaning that we knew they'd understand.

Standing silently for a few seconds, we used our focus to remotely put the image inside it. It stopped. Motionless and directly above, it flashed one momentary light at us. We jumped and cheered like ten-year old's, laughing, and saying, "It sees us, oh my god, it stopped!". After its brief pause above us, it continued to float on its wobbly way.

This then affirms that they are masters of their minds to receive our information instantly and remotely. As many sources have attested, they operate their craft using telepathy, or are at least attached by their physical body, to connect information from their brains to parts of the vehicle. This suggests incredible singularity of thought among the collective. If they weren't cohesively in control of their minds to operate the craft by thought and intent, then they'd be scattered all over the place. Everyone onboard must have the same objective, and wholeness in consciousness to keep the craft moving to its destination. And to have our message received in a moment also affirms the timelessness of reality. Our message didn't travel, it was there instantly, which means we also accessed the non-local Void for it to appear to them.

I decided to stop the excessive work I'd dived into. I was obviously incapable of thinking through it from the beginning, and I abruptly withdrew. It was after this that other revelations about me were arrived at in the space provided. It's not to say my symptoms went away. I had continued numbness on my left most of the time; and got dizziness and panic when at the shops, or if friends talked too much and I felt compelled to pretend I was okay. To avoid this, I forced myself to spend a lot of time at home, where my mind had small opportunities to evaluate myself and my predicament. One thing resulted from this, which led me to the sweetest conclusion about my purpose in life, and again turned me back to accessing my mind, and resuming my disciplines.

A graceful learning came from finally understanding something Ram said that I never quite got: about seeing things as they really are. In my misunderstanding, I thought this may mean we interpret events or people's intentions incorrectly. Giving myself space to reflect, I got one of those mysterious and sudden knowingness's that I described earlier. It wasn't other people's actions or events – it

Chapter 13: The Wobble

was mine. It is always about us if there is a problem, and the answers always lay in us too.

I could never see my honest motivations for doing things. The perpetual strain was because I was insisting on false truths I forced on myself and others, which was like trying to swim against choking rapids while kicking underwater boulders. Whilst it sounds cliché, it's a befitting visual for living in contradictions. As an example, I never recognised my true intentions for marrying until writing this book. I'd convinced myself that my husband deceived me, used me, and hurt me. The truth of the matter was that I had felt embarrassed being single in my twenties, and I was jealous of couples who had more than me. I couldn't see things as they really were.

I also wanted to be a Head of Department, but not because I felt ready to after two decades in the classroom. I saw that people on higher pay in my profession put all their work on teachers who were over-extended already, and their resumes for moving upward relied on fads they passed onto us to design and implement. When the bell went, we stuffed food in our mouths and ran to get our laptops while they sat leisurely laughing together at the lunch table. I had decided the only way out of this avalanche of work was to have what they had.

After coming clean on my denial, I felt an increased sense of ease more regularly, and although my body was yet to catch up, there was a notable subduing of frenzied energy felt.

CHAPTER FOURTEEN

The Mother Ship

Post divorce, I'd been so drained that I couldn't see my youngest daughter was sliding into her own abyss. Puberty had been unkind to her, and circumstances living part-time between each parent contributed to her physical ill-health and depression. Sadly, my absence through work and inability to cope compounded these things for her, and her dad's culture cemented them too.

In Egypt, having chubby children is a symbol of wealth and success, where the whole country bar a few live in abject poverty. Having fat kids means you're a good provider, and clearly have money. Unfortunately, however, they don't have the education to go with contemporary dietary research. My husband was told by his doctor in Egypt that a lady's period is a rotten egg coming out, and he was told beer burns holes in your stomach lining where it then leaks into your abdomen to slush around, hence the size of drinker's bellies. This should indicate the level of health advice seemingly educated people get. As such, my girl was fed thick shakes, burgers, fries, cookies, chocolate – you name it.

In another time and place, a full figure may be a measure of success, but on the Gold Coast where people value sculpted physiques, she struggled with a poor self-image. She also inherited her

Chapter 14: The Mother Ship

Arabian grandmother's breasts, that are far too large for her narrow ribcage. Having a size K cup (it may help to say the alphabet from A to K to understand the size), has not been easy on her.

This was not the least of her pain, however, as we discovered her dad had been punching and threatening her over the years since we'd separated. Whilst we made an initial police report after she told me, when it went higher for investigation, she was afraid of getting him in trouble and denied it all. According to her, he'd always warn her she'd never see him again, and be dead to him. She both loves and fears him.

He also supplied her drugs and alcohol, and the ramifications for that were secrecy after the cops got a denial from him. To be fair though, through interviews with police he has become aware that using fear and forceful compliance won't be ignored by me, and he has stopped the corporal punishment. At least that's what I'm led to believe. He does adore her, and as his only living relative on Earth, he doesn't want to lose her.

Before these revelations, in 2016 I mustered the courage to take her with me on an overseas trip. I use 'courage', because after losing a fortune in the pre-divorce proceedings, I went away for six weeks relying only on the credit card. I can describe most of it as an ordeal, because when you're in foreign countries you have no security when you don't know your bearings, or what time places close for food or fuel, and I didn't just have myself to worry about if I got lost. She was a little champion for her mum, being my navigator using the smartphone maps while I drove. I had no idea how to use Bluetooth then, so her job was to tell me every turn while I drove around the entire UK for the first half of the holiday.

One of the purposes of the trip was to find a crop circle in the UK. I know there are many fakes, but if you're unfamiliar, have a quick search and make a quick evaluation of the intricate ones. There's no way these babies could be faked without trampling the surrounds during measuring and calculation. Ram had told us the image of the alien with the pipe, on this book's cover, was made by his people. He said they didn't look like this, but it was a recognisable image to demonstrate they weren't from this world. The smoking, too, is deliberate. Tobacco without the chemicals is not dangerous, and in fact we have receptor sites for it. It increases focus and opens the brain where it is otherwise quiet, to tap into the deeper regions and make contact with ourselves.

We visited the site of the smoking alien, which was no longer visible of course, and spent the next six hours looking for a new one. Sometimes I'm a little slow in my uptake – I could have searched online for recent ones and sought them out, but me being me, I relied on impulsiveness and drove us around all day looking. There's another problem searching in this way: fields everywhere in this region have high hedges. After generating sufficient guilt for dragging my kid needlessly across Wiltshire, and a hundred F bombs getting lost – I gave up.

"Bugger it", I said, "Let's just stop here at this burial site and have a walk". Blow me down! As soon as I stood out of the car, I was looking straight at a crop circle! It'd been mowed over, but given its flat design in the wheat, it was beautifully unmarked. We ran directly to the design, and were the only ones there to explore it. I noted its folded and unbroken stems, with the expanded nodes at the bends. Each shaft was meticulously swirled, forming a visible shadow effect in different areas of the diagram, for optimum optics. I opened my messenger app to ring my eldest daughter, and it would not ring. I tried several times to no avail, and instead focussed on taking pictures. It had no problems ringing after we exited it, however, telling indeed. Silbury Hill appeared behind it too, making the whole scenario very mystical.

In the years following, I attempted to have one or two nights away with my youngest daughter most school holidays. We would go

Chapter 14: The Mother Ship

camping, and in quiet moments I'd chat about personal growth in an effort to help her turn inward for her will and strength. I'd certainly not been a perfect model of it, but it was better than speaking shit about nothing.

One afternoon of camping, we were talking about the grid while we sat beside a lovely man-made dam. She'd been to two retreats as a kid and had sufficient training to know the lingo and engage in the conversation; and she's a deep one who has shown a tendency to philosophise since she was small. The sun was placed above the distant mountains when we noted something unusual. "What the hell is that?", I asked in my usual antipodean manner. It was something very enormous situated next to the sun, at the same elevation above the mountains.

It must've been fricken huge! The mountains were far away in the distance, but this thing was big and wide enough that we could still see rows of coloured lights horizontally across its middle. It was almost the same height as the sun, but slightly wider than it. At that distance and placement near the horizon, the heat or energy on the Earth somewhat distorted the image, so it was not entirely clearcut for distinguishing its features. We sat for a few minutes wondering if its location would change, to indicate if we were watching a plane or not. It didn't. In fact, it remained stationary for so long that we could see the sun slowly descending beside it while it remained in the same position above the mountains.

It was daytime, and not yet any hint of dusk approaching. We articulated to each other what we were seeing, and noted its burger shape – huge, considering its distance from us, and proximity to the sun. The lights must've been very intense, as their sparkling effect obscured a portion of what we were observing. It remained unmoving, so we ruled out any conventional plane, which from its size, shape, and lighting, was not hard to do.

After about fifteen minutes of staring, I ran to get my mobile phone to film it. Normally these occurrences were so fleeting it would have been pointless to waste the moments opening my camera. In the past, I never had my phone on me to think to take pictures – and honestly, you're so stunned in those moments you simply don't think. This occasion was distinctly different. I tried to take pictures and videos of this giant craft, but none of them showed it. Thankfully it was sitting there for so long I could stop, zoom, check, change the zoom or remove it. None of them captured it. I still don't know why, perhaps the distance or the brightness of the sun.

We continued to sit there watching, even until the sun had disappeared, and dusk emerged. Still, the huge burger remained in its position. Lights glistening across it, with the backdrop of the sun now behind the mountain, its shape was still well defined.

As darkness began, the huge ship's lights were brighter without the sun present, and the shape of the craft was somehow illuminated around it for it to be visible. Ever so slowly it started to move at a forty-five-degree angle to its upper right. It didn't tilt, and this slow movement lasted at least thirty minutes. From this higher position in the sky, we could then determine it began to face away from Earth as it exited our atmosphere. This process of moving away took a really long time, if I'm to compare it to the blink it took for others to ping out of sight, and it grew smaller in size as it withdrew. The lights, however, did not diminish. In fact, I could say they looked more like a thrust effect – coming off its base like flames. This too seemed to last twenty to thirty minutes.

I don't believe size makes any difference to these majestic craft. Just because we think enormous things are harder to move and need more combustion, doesn't mean these ones do. That's our conditioned assumptions; similar to other limited ones held by academics, like searching for Goldy Locks planets that are just right for humans. Conventional scientists suggest that just because we live in these conditions then all infinite life must do so. Reject conventional science in this case, and the notion that size matters regarding agility of movement. Assuming other life rely on propellants to create energy for movement is such an outdated concept.

Chapter 14: The Mother Ship

I've seen a variety of craft manoeuvre like nothing else, and I don't buy the standard physics that larger is harder. No doubt mine sitting close to me were all much smaller, but remember one wasn't even solid in its skin, and don't forget the monster outside my daughter's window, which I didn't see while sitting directly underneath it! Who knows why it exited unbelievably slow. Given that it was able to defy gravity for so long, I don't expect it had any difficulty moving out to space because of its size. Maybe it was for maximum viewing by many people. We will one day find out.

CHAPTER FIFTEEN

The Red Lights

In the years separated from my husband, the idea emerged that perhaps I'd never made myself attractive enough for the men in my life. I hadn't had many, but there were often remarks about my lack of presentation over the decades.

Introduced to enlightenment at nineteen, I concluded men could all love me outside of my appearance, after all, wasn't that what love really was? I'd convinced myself I was satisfied being a natural looking girl, barely wearing a stitch of makeup or colouring my hair. Giving in to concepts of grooming myself to be attractive to my men seemed like selling myself out, and I always wanted to model character as my strength to my daughters. Truth be told, my tummy and boobs were so stretched from breastfeeding and pregnancy I looked like I'd had a roll in the sack with Freddy Kruger, so didn't have the confidence to engage with men I preferred. Facing being older and alone, I understood I'd only *tried* not being concerned with my body image.

When I was married, I occasionally wondered why I never received one hint of a compliment. And I mean nothing. Didn't men normally say something encouraging to their wives? I wasn't butt ugly, and I remember asking once if there was anything in particular

Chapter 15: The Red Lights

he liked about me. My skin? My face? Anything? His exact reply was, "Be glad I don't notice these things in you, or I'd notice younger and prettier". I stared stunned for a moment and didn't know how to respond. Perhaps, I justified, this meant he wasn't superficial, and that was a good thing. Only, after discovering the prolific span and regularity of his sleeping around, it seemed he was doing exactly that.

My three-year onslaught with the neighbour similarly included how ugly and fat I was. The latter was definitely true: I had grown fat. On occasions people asked when my baby was due, and I empathised with their embarrassment when I said I wasn't expecting – more than I faced my own. I had never experienced having a loving relationship, and in the vacuum of my empty mind I thus applied my discipline to changing myself physically. I lost around thirty kilos of weight through fasting, and had a tummy tuck and my baggy eyelids trimmed after the weight loss made everything droopy. On the surface, I convinced myself fasting was to increase my longevity, which placated my intellect, and I provided myself the illusion of being in control when I'd felt so powerless. I had utterly given in to the last vestige of my humanity to find worth, again to out-source it from others.

I wonder now, how much of a failure I made my youngest daughter feel. She shaved her hair off and insisted she was a boy in the wrong body, painfully strapping her breasts down and wearing men's clothes. The barrage of teasing and isolation this elicited in her early years of high school were unbearable, yet she persisted as stubbornly as I was starving myself. To what extent was her self-rejection my doing, given her budding femininity emerged when her mum was half her size at eleven and twelve? How far the pendulum swings when we are separated from our divine selves. No wonder I had no off-world visitors for a period: there was nothing worth stopping for.

Predictably, I decided to try online dating. I'd been single most of my twenties because I wanted something meaningful, which never materialised, and I didn't want another decade of waiting since I was on the far end of my youthful bloom. It was uncomfortable to me that people pick from a catalogue of images – such an unnatural way to meet – and it never occurred to me it might also be full of vipers in relationships, essentially leading single women on to distract from the lack of effort to their own. I was too drained to be choosy, though, so after only a couple of interactions, I met my fella, whom I was living with while writing this book.

He is an incredibly hard worker, and I always appreciated his endurance. If I needed jobs done at my house, he did them impeccably, which I'd offset against his lack of affection or mindful interest in me. Often, I would try to generate meaningful conversation and he would interject over me on his own tangent, like I hadn't spoken. Since I'd never had anyone who did things for me before, I was constantly persuading myself not to be critical, yet despite my justifications, a sense of being invisible always prevailed.

For the thirteen years with my husband, I lived in the duality of trying to be enlightened while covering up the monumental lies of my life. Naturally, I could never decipher truth, and the confusion flowed into this scenario too. I persevered, as I was a teacher with a learnt ethos of never giving up on people, particularly the rough and uncultured ones, who always warmed my heart. This inner conflict, a residue of my childhood, would eventually become the drive for learning to differentiate between the knowing Observer and the conditioned attitudes that clouded my understanding. But, not without a lot of pain in doing so.

Before commencing with this project, I sat with the idea of writing the book for a few weeks. For once in my life, I didn't act impulsively and crash right in. I let the idea settle, and gave my head space to nut out the pros and cons.

Chapter 15: The Red Lights

One evening, I was sitting quite late on my bedroom balcony to quiet myself in readiness to do a discipline, having a smoke. I adore the silence at night, and I'm ordinarily gazing upwards at the stars – beauty that they are – determining what my focus will be. On this occasion, however, I was distracted by two small, intense red lights.

They were near the top of my small back fence, about three or four inches apart, and probably a couple of inches each in size. The left one was slightly bigger than the right, but not noticeably so. Staring for a minute without thinking anything of them, and daydreaming about whether to do this book, I realised the sight was a bit odd. I looked up at my neighbour's house because I knew the kids had a coloured nightlight in their bedroom, but I kind of knew it wouldn't cast two red lights this far across our yards, especially in distinct finite shapes as they were. I then wondered if they were shining red lights my way to play tricks on me, but it was too late for them to be awake, and their house had been silent and dark for a while anyway. When I looked back, the red lights had gone. I searched with my eyes for a bit, wanting to see them again – or at least figure out their origin – to no avail.

Then I remembered a picture I'd seen from Ramtha's school. Two red lights in a white plasma shape had been caught on digital camera at the top corner of the arena where people attended for teachings. Ram said it was Mothman. My automatic response to wondering if this was him was to become suddenly frightened. I caught myself quickly, however, because I don't want to reject these possibilities. From my experiences with craft present, I'd never been frightened because one does not equate craft with beings when you aren't seeing them. I bluffed myself that Mothman was much bigger than us, and his eyes wouldn't be four feet from the ground, in an effort to calm down. Besides that, I continued, he was warning people of danger, so surely, I have no reason to be afraid. I explored other possibilities in my head for the red lights, and concluding nothing, I went inside.

Roughly two weeks later, I was sitting in my small backyard, again pondering about writing this book. My boyfriend was chit chatting, and my habit of losing attention – except when I'm working – ensued. While he spoke, I was staring at a shrub near to where the first two lights were seen, and not for the purpose of seeing them as I had temporarily forgotten them, when the red lights reappeared. Strangely, and again absentmindedly, I was just staring at them, unregistering their presence. I was mesmerised by their gentle rhythmic flicker and the red brilliance emanating from a dense core, when I realised I was staring at the same mysterious lights. It was daylight, so no causal reflection was apparent from anything that might be the case at night, lending me to suspect they were car reverse lights – but I was in a garden with a plush shrub, fence, and trees behind them. Realising that, I did what I do when UFOs show up – I stared to absorb every single detail.

This pair were again spaced the same distance as the first set, but were more brilliant and intense. When we look at a source of light in the day there is usually a dulling effect because of the light around, but not in this case. They were producing multiple, slow-moving shapes of vivid red, like seaweed appears under water, from what looked to be a square source. I couldn't see them emanating from every side, nor from their rear, only forwards with some splaying outward; and the left one was again brighter, and slightly larger. It had the sense of being electronic, if I was to liken it to something, but there was no visible device, per se, as to what was generating it.

I then had the thought they were associated with the writing of the book. As soon as I thought this, they ceased. Gone entirely in a moment, not fading out. I went over and knelt by the place they were in, to see if I could see anything there. My boyfriend wondered what I was doing. I gave a brief account, but by the way he quickly returned to his one-sided conversation, I knew he didn't consider it discussion worthy. That was okay, after all I was disinterested in his conversation too. I also know that in other's shoes they're dismissive when they haven't had supernatural experiences.

I decided then that I had to do this. I also wondered if my brain was beginning to see things from doing grid regularly again. When

Chapter 15: The Red Lights

I'd done the candle discipline for months every night, I saw strange things too. This wasn't sustained at the time, as I got frightened of what else I might see and gave it up. The things we do when we're not mature!

Thus decided, I made a start. I also made enquiries about publishing and searched online for similar authors to ask for their advice on this. I didn't take long locating Dr Michael Salla from *Exopolitics*, and I had a read of his credentials. I was certain he wouldn't bother reading emails from the public, after all, he might get hundreds – good, bad, or nut job! Surprisingly, I discovered he had been an academic nearby in Queensland where my eldest daughter had just graduated. Being Australian and an educator, I felt a kinship so to speak, and a little less shy in asking him.

To my delight he replied in a couple of days. He said to publish it myself online and directed me where to start. In his kind reply, he asked if I had photos to give credibility to my audience. I hadn't thought of that, and the answer was no. I'd never taken my phone out for focus before, and to be honest, I wouldn't have caught any anyway. They stay for such a brief moment, and there's no way I'm taking my eyes off them to fiddle with the phone and bring it up. There's too much astonishment, and too much to absorb, but I also never seriously considered writing a book to one day need photos. I decided then I would start doing grid outside with my phone, as I'd been doing it solely in my room.

I did this for two nights and gave up. There's no authentic focus when you're sitting there waiting with a phone in hand, and this would be assuming they come on my terms. At any rate, I wanted genuine recovery, as well as a better future, and I was finally accepting that I could have it with dedicated focus. I care more about my enlightenment than I do having UFOs present, as weird as that may sound.

Regarding my experiences with craft, since resuming the disciplines, I have occasionally included one area of interest to me. In focus, I go back in time to each UFO that was present and touch the craft's skin, using the grid as an overlay. Abstractly, my touching signifies connecting me with them to know about our relationship to one another, and why they have shown themselves. It's also to demonstrate my acceptance and willingness to have further contact, even if some have differing biology to my own.

Of interest, I had a stunning realisation. I'd wondered about being tracked over my life, mostly from the repeated visits by the gold disk and the silver boomerang. It's occurred to me years after the fact, naturally, considering my emotional distraction, that the bottom of the gold skinned craft would be a round gold disk. It was too low for me to see at the time, and my eyes were also focussed on the black portholes, but picturing the dense gold light of the body it would make sense that it was exactly what I'd seen in the nineties, and the one floating over me in my present house. It had come three times, and that was just the times I'd seen it!

Going forward, however, I have chosen not to use the word tracked, as this seems to carry a detached connotation of experimentation. It also implies a one-sided interaction. I don't think relationships with spiritually advanced people are one-sided, not when we understand the wholeness of all existence. I think there's a mutual reciprocation between them and myself for our meetings. Instead, I prefer to think they are propelling me to carry on for my enlightenment using the disciplines, and possibly for writing this book.

CHAPTER SIXTEEN

The Flash

Another area of focus has been my union with the silent observer in me; the thing that has always peered through my eyes, alluded to near the start of this book. For over twenty years of participation in Ramtha's school, I always thought of this eternal thing as the God in me, but not *me*. Sometimes over the years, I had practiced aligning myself with it but not had much success sustaining this because I was convinced its presence was separate from myself, meaning me as my personality. I figured my intent of desiring union would be recognised by this silent essence, until gradually it would meld with me.

Instead, during the early stages of writing this book, I had a sudden and beautiful realisation: *It* is me. It's me without the disruption. This may seem obvious for others, but for me this was everything to do with worth. I don't think I was capable of thinking that huge eternal force, the source of all possibilities, could be me. And, strangely, after having this simple understanding, I no longer struggled aligning with it – I began just being it. It came very easily, surprisingly, but holding my focus steady in this state needed further integration.

I thus began practising shifting from my personality to the quiet, unjudging self before engaging in my disciplines. In saying this though, I'd been so distracted by anxiety that my mind was still extremely scattered, and holding a singular image was difficult. The key for me was to not get upset at the two second interruptions, and just chill and move back into focus. Again, and again, and again.

I'd given myself the year to master my mind and health, and in so doing, dedicated myself to diving back into the disciplines. How I sacrificed these for slave labour over the decades when I had so much evidence they worked, is beyond me. Nevertheless, I was back on.

With brain frazzled from cortisol for years, I had a strong inclination to be cocooned in my bedroom for focus in the beginning. I knew I had to be outside to see any craft, but I cared more about creating a future that didn't take me back to where I'd been. I'd lost my ability to hold extended focus, and being so used to pushing myself for work, I even had trouble disconnecting from writing this book in every moment. I would go to sit still, put on music with my set image in mind, then start rattling sentences off to include here. Disconnecting from my thinking brain needed perseverance, which improved at a snail's pace incrementally.

At the time, I listened to a podcast by JZ, who channels Ram, and she reminded me of something I'd forgotten. She explained that when we ask a question, the spirit interacts on the neurons to stimulate a future experience for it to be answered. This was worthy of contemplation for me, and I wondered if I always needed to have a new opportunity for the answers to things, or if I had already had them and overlooked the wisdom therein.

Similarly, given the countless lives lived through reincarnation, we've likely experienced everything one could possibly do for learning that exists here. The problem is: during our life, truth is obscured by powerful repetitive emotions that prevent us from seeing things as they really are. And, once we've died and seen the truth on the other side, we are compelled to get it right next time, only to be reborn

Chapter 16: The Flash

with amnesia and risk missing another opportunity. With guidance and training, however, we can reconnect with that wisdom quietly residing in the soul.

How many lives have I died and returned to being a victim and attempted to source love from other people? By asking the subtle questions I have discovered the Observer can deliver the knowledge from what is already stored, hence my flashes of knowingness and the occasional audible messages. Furthermore, we could also pull it from the future. If our Observer is outside of linear time, then we can access it from our future experiences. This may be a stretch for us, but seeing the ability of UFOs to appear exactly when I'm doing disciplines suggests they knew ahead when and where I'd be – which can only be known stepping in and out of time.

As an example, I asked why I kept waiting for people who don't care about me to love me. Not long later, I spontaneously heard the sentence in my head, "Because you are stuck trying to find it from the original source, your mother". Obvious in hindsight now, this revelation was extraordinary to me. We have difficulty seeing the characteristics we occupy, but when we ask the question, we are essentially standing outside of the issue and looking at it.

Just as JZ discussed, the subtle spirit also delivered a random documentary to corroborate this only days later. It described what psychology calls *arrested development*, where the original trauma is forever acting out the earlier experience to find redemption. I won't compare myself to the eight-year-old mind of Michael Jackson in the doco, of course, but it afforded hints indicating the same concept.

The experience of hearing audible responses has rarely occurred in my life, being usually only flashes of knowingness or floating imagery in the background of my awareness. When I have had it, it is curiously on the left side of my head that I hear it, if you can call it hearing. Perhaps having the time to contemplate was the precursor I had never given myself. Which raises the topic of contemplation.

Often on my own, I drift into repetitive thinking and can be hijacked for hours or days, only to elicit stress and more confusion. People say they need closure, but is it really because we cannot still the mind to find the answers within so seek people and situations to fill the gaps? By contemplating, I have recently deduced, we instead offer a gentle query to our observer and await the answer. Whilst the issue can still be pressing at times, there is no angst, most likely because it is the genuine seeking of wisdom and comes from a place of honesty. This is the best way I can decipher the two anyway.

Dedicating my time to contemplation and disciplines, I slowly began to understand that I've spent my whole life trying to find validation from everything externally. I naturally never found it in relationships or work, and even then, I only gave so I would be given. Like the T-shirt that says, "I found Jesus, he was under the lounge the whole time", I was always being redirected back to myself, where worth, love and security have resided all along.

Reflecting on myself, I recalled my ex-husband's confidence and self-worth when he'd been a loser in my eyes. It's because he was loved unconditionally by his single mum, and therefore wasn't programmed to have any qualifiers for it. True worth shouldn't, as our very existence is testimony of, and only we judge who deserves it by our conditioning.

Of the many questions I am constantly asking, the 'whys' regarding the presence of UFOs has often been one of them. On the surface, I've been a general fuck up to myself, and yet a variety of different craft, and presumably diverse races, have taken moments in their life to affirm I was onto something. This leads me to postulate their appearances could possibly concern the readers of this book. I've included many inferences to futures being known in this text, given the preciseness of craft's appearances, so I'm now wondering if these beings have made themselves visible for a known outcome arising

Chapter 16: The Flash

from its publication. This possibility may be more readily accepted if we compare ET contact types.

Today there are groups meeting to contact extra-terrestrials using consciousness protocols with genuinely encouraging results. But what was the difference in having several stationary, close-range observers as opposed to distant flashes and bright stars sailing overhead that the other protocols elicit? In my opinion, it's this: I never once sought contact. What I did, however, was seek contact with the Source *in* me, for self-deliverance. And, if I recall correctly from Dr Greer's earlier books, so were his initial contacts with beings and craft in his younger years. He was practicing meditations – essentially turning inward – and they showed up close and personally for him too.

Accessing individual divinity in a larger number of people may be the after effect of this book, as perhaps many may be compelled to engage practices after reading this. I already suspect that people who contemplate something greater in them, and additionally, those doing concerted efforts to awaken themselves, are being watched. The craft and its occupants are perhaps not showing themselves based on the individual's readiness, or perhaps people have simply not entertained this concept enough to hardwire seeing them.

To one day intermingle with evolved beings, we need to find the will to help ourselves. If we mastered our propensity for operating on emotional biology, we'd be clean and transparent in our relations with them. I sometimes laughed with my boyfriend about the telepathy ETs purportedly use, picturing the chaos we'd have here if everyone's thoughts were audible! Imagine the calibre of mind these beings must have to communicate peacefully and collectively to get where they're at.

Towards the latter end of 2022, I was often overwhelmed by my body's numbness and nerve pain in both legs, and sometimes both forearms, particularly at night. You can imagine how these constant sensations can be terrifying, and oftentimes I was on the edge of hysterical fear about developing a disease. I went outside one evening to prepare for focus, and not surprisingly, I was horribly distracted and deflated. Unexpectedly, I heard clearly in my head, 'I have an indomitable spirit'. When I don't think these things deliberately, I know they are straight from the divine part of me.

Just as this audible message occurred, a large and brilliant light turned on directly in my gaze. Positioned stationary above the tree line, and seemingly only a couple of hundred metres away, its intensity instantly stole my attention. Then it flashed. One brief burst, unmistakably right at me. Its incandescence, like a blazing white sun, made it impossible to see the craft that produced it.

It was a full moon, so the night sky was dark blue as opposed to black, making visibility unobscured, and only a few vaporous clouds interrupted the peppering of stars. Remaining lit long enough to note a regular plane gliding above in tiny contrast, it then floated slowly to my left a bit before blipping completely out. The clear night did not show any unlit object fly out of view – it was simply not there.

I was so pleased. It'd been years since I saw my interdimensional friends; and again, engaging in my disciplines proved to be paying off. The craft and its occupants knew my worry, and knew I needed inspiration. It wasn't they who had sent the instant message, as the voice in my head had used *I*, but they were on cue to appear when I needed affirmation.

This beautifully timed appearance, and the revelation that the gold disk had shown up at least three times, must be an acknowledgement of my divine worth to uncloak for. It also means they have never judged my actions and inadequacies, and instead, understand that every experience delivers wisdom eventually. Their appearances for me are demonstrations of a love I have not yet understood, and I will hold onto these notions as truth because issues of self-worth and seeking love motivated me all along. They will be my reminder to source it *in me*.

Chapter 16: The Flash

I felt I was nearing the end of my book by this stage; and similarly concluded I'd incurred enough of what doesn't kill you to get on with increasing the capacity of my mind, when something else began to unfold. Instead, it seemed the poker hadn't been hot enough thus far – and it was about to turn red.

CHAPTER SEVENTEEN

The Giant

Parallel to writing, I had begun to withdraw from my man, as I wanted to use the time more in my application of the disciplines. He was always on his phone anyway, and our conversations were usually one-way. This wasn't well received, as he'd been used to my ever-giving expenditure of energy towards him.

He was always a drinker and occasional weed user, but this increased considerably from the void I created, and at times he'd yell at me when I voiced my discontent at his behaviours. The unpredictability and fear of escalation was also impacting on my health. Often, he wouldn't remember his actions when raised the next day and insisted I was making things up. I couldn't get through to him, and to avoid the embarrassment of neighbours hearing, I would sit there when he came and ranted – braced, silent, and angry.

These incidences occurred more frequently when I received word my work insurance was coming to an end, of which I can only speculate was because I was regularly hiding in my room – petrified for my future. The gripping fear of not being able to support myself with half-bodied numbness and horrible anxiety intensified my symptoms. The paraesthesia spread from my arms and legs and into my spine. The very real terror of thinking I was dying of something thus

Chapter 17: The Giant

made focus near impossible, and despite the true power of focus I espouse here – I was facing the real challenge of putting my truth to the test.

Resentful at becoming the dutiful pseudo-housewife, sitting every afternoon to hear repetitive stories of who'd done this or that at work, and who was plotting against him, I had started to rebel. I hated his constant self-interest and lack of shared intellectual conversations that would contribute to any bond or personal growth, and concluded I'd done it again: overlooked red flags, and seamlessly taken on being the sub-servient, self-sacrificer.

During these months, my condition turned more wicked, and buzzing began all over my body for the duration of the night. It was like being plugged into voltage and supercharging every single nerve, from my neck to the ends of my limbs. Absolutely terrifying. It kept me from sleeping, and I often paused this book because my nerves would hurt all day as a consequence.

One morning, in the hours before waking, I had a hideous nightmare. Ram said dreams for the first few hours of the night were the seemingly nonsensical ones for healing the body, and the ones before waking were the prophetic type that made sense of the world and our interactions with them.

The dream literally woke me in fitful torment from the struggle therein. I must've been dreaming of the very real agony, but within it lay a deep, subconscious reckoning where I was fighting to pull a demonic type entity out of my thighs and pelvic region. As weird as that sounds, and not meaning to have religious connotations, it was that frightening. Although it wasn't tangible, I was trying to wrench the creature out of my body using my mind, much like an exorcism. Its appearance was gnarled and screaming; its face grimacing as it struggled to remain, unrelenting. It was multiple shades of grey and white in its apparition, female too, and the intensity eventually woke me. The first realisation was that the contorted face was mine. I instantly determined it to be the angry, powerless victim in me that had materialised in the nervous condition I was facing.

One night shortly after, my boyfriend saw me laying on the floor feeling quietly overcome. Glancing dismissively at me, he turned to lay on the bed and play a game on his phone. The cheerful whirs, buzz and pings from it aptly juxtaposed my silent rage. I made the decision he had to go, and fearfully expressed it to him. He was adamant he wasn't going anywhere, so I involved the police.

My youngest daughter had stopped living at my house by then, and I was ashamed of losing another daughter's respect over my choices of men. I'd been ignorant of the extent of my own powerlessness at the onset of the relationship and was decidedly focused on restoring it. After all, I was writing a book about conquering one's bullshit, so I had to be accountable for my words here too.

I decided I was never going to bite my tongue again.

In the days that followed I opened an older teaching of Ram's about why our bodies grow old and sick. In it, he discussed the habits of the personality affecting our health, and this included our relationships. Having my debilitating paraesthesia, I knew if I didn't stop repeating these situations, I would be slowly killing myself.

After my boyfriend left, he revealed he'd started chatting to someone on a dating app, saying I'd made him feel stupid all the time. Knowing I had his emails open on the laptop he'd given me to write this, my curiosity got the better of me. I convinced myself they were already open and didn't need a login, and that it wasn't too unethical to take a look. This marked the beginning of a war in me, and as one can predict, for him too.

I typed different dating app names in the search and was absolutely floored. He'd been doing this on and off over the five-year duration of the relationship, not just in the days before leaving as he'd claimed. I couldn't believe this man, whom had been cheated on himself many times before me and knew my husband had done so irreverently for thirteen years, could have done this. After all,

Chapter 17: The Giant

he knew his own pain and mine; and I'd also done so much to help him when others hadn't, was stalwartly loyal, and was by no means a seahag by then either. Fuck, I couldn't win. At least not in the regular material sense.

I'd never once had cause to doubt him – he was always with me. I couldn't read the messages between many women occurring simultaneously, as they were notifications saying he'd "received a new reply" or "It's a match!", and so forth. I could not recall one occasion where he'd slipped out of the house or acted suspiciously, and I surmised he must've been just texting countless women for the flattery and titillation.

Torturing myself, I perused through photos of us on my phone and matched the dates with his varying chats across the dating platforms. I couldn't escape my devastation and disbelief that happier moments were occurring while he was sweet talking women, and possibly exchanging erotic images and sex talk. My shock at the extent of the betrayal was beyond words. I was literally receiving the icing on the cake of my poor me life story – and I'd thought while writing this book I'd had it all. Although, somehow, this time it didn't have the same feel as being the victim.

Spending January 2023 crying incessantly, I withdrew from everyone except my parents, who came at different times to check on me because all I could do over the phone was scream-cry. I spent every day rotating between laying on the carpet howling to forcefully doing disciplines in an attempt to eradicate the misery. The relentless, hard crying was a real puzzle to me. I'd never experienced this reaction to any man before, and I scolded myself for being so ruined by one.

Ramtha once mentioned the tale of Dante in the inferno from *The Divine Comedy*, a story I haven't read, but am familiar enough to know. It's an allegory of one's uncovering of self, where Dante is accompanied through hell by Virgil the poet, obviously the metaphor for his divine self. Inferno is a befitting word for this process.

Getting to the core of truth about ourselves is agony, and often we walk through things that scorch us, over and over and over.

In my few months of total meltdown, I was torn trying to decipher between two minds. On the one hand there was my primitive feminine self, rejected again and hating this man's guts for chasing other women; and on the other, my divine observer objectively reminding me there is no moral high ground in the quantum field, and my experiences were all purposeful. No prizes for guessing which side would win that battle.

I had another interesting dream during this that could not have been more pertinent to myself. Always take note of the dreams before waking, they're often revelatory. In it, I came across the character of Gollum from *Lord of the Rings*, burning in a fire outside in the woods. He was inside a closed black oven with a glass door, and I could see he was writhing in agony. Knowing that Gollum was a hideous character, that represented our shadow selves and deserved to die, I still felt sorry for it dying this way, and quickly pulled him out. Crimson coloured from exposed flesh, I determined the best thing was to smash his head in with a nearby rock to end his suffering. I held the rock up – but couldn't do it. I let him scamper painfully out of sight. This was my own reticence to end my hidden demons, and I did exactly as I had in my dream: ignored what I knew to do.

I entered a bitter wrath and set about punishing my ex via text and email. He, on the other hand, sent messages of love, realising his behaviours were cruel and devastating. He even sent a song called *Hate Me* that was a close account of us. God, I really cried. When he finally began to ignore me, I discovered a part of myself that was very confronting.

I sent what on the surface was an honest message, acknowledging how I'd always made him feel less intelligent, and likely made him feel inadequate over the years. It was true, I used my intellectualism in conversations to try to expand his thinking, but I guess it

Chapter 17: The Giant

made him feel his responses weren't as wise as mine. Receiving this, he softened and responded gently. I felt the rush of power in me – he'd given in so easily. I could see I'd used honesty when I was losing his connection and had resorted to a manipulative tactic.

As the spirit would have it, ever patient and prodding, I stumbled on a podcast with a snippet pertinent to my behaviours. Joe Rogan was interviewing an academic, an esteemed doctor whose name I don't recall right now, who brought up the psychology of women. Here he described how *Beauty and the Beast* represented women's desire to change men as their most basic drive. I had taught enough literature in my years to also recognise that the rose symbol in the story, where Belle must end the curse before it withers and dies, was representative of a women's youth and beauty – pointing also to the primitive weakness in men. Women were influential as long as they were lovely, or sexually attractive, more accurately. Obviously my petals had already dropped.

I'd been tormenting him for over six weeks, and was confused about whether I actually loved him to be doing this, or if this was my hurt pride and anger at being invisible again. I'd compromised my values for my physical image, and none of it had made a tinker's damn. He wasn't innocent, as he had countless opportunities over the years to appreciate he had a decent girl and pull his head in, but his persistence was flattering, and I wanted respite from my grief to get clarity.

I decided to let him back in.

On the surface we had a pleasant night; despite horrendous anxiety I felt every time his phone pinged and he responded – the insecurity was killing me. I eventually sat in the other room crying till dawn while he slept like a baby. When I expressed it the next morning, he volunteered his phone for me to go through. Knowing he'd pre-emptively deleted anything incriminating, I still said yes.

My god: what happened next was crushing. If I hadn't walked through the valley of death the last two months, I certainly did after this. I stumbled on a dot above his messages called 'recycle bin'. Therein I found the sordid details no already tormented woman ever wants to see. I saw into his soul, and the secret lives men and women have when they are outright debased. I could see there were countless number of them, but after reading three or four I couldn't keep my trap shut. He'd said he never met anyone or had any encounters, as one would do when they're trying to rekindle something.

After mouthing off what I'd read, I asked sarcastically if he was embarrassed, deliberately to belittle him. I could see in his eyes that my posture and expression made him unsure of what I might do next, and he quickly gathered his keys and items to leave. When I asked twice if he was going to collect his music equipment on the way out, he was aptly reading my mind. I had fleeting images of taking an axe to it all.

Ensuing weeks of self-destruction followed, as I faced my biggest battle. Despite the raging emotions, I was always seeing the simultaneous truth from a divine perspective. He'd had a lifetime of neglect and abuse and had never been modelled love or care from his parents. As an example, in his early teenage years, his dad had ordered an older brother to shoot his dog Girly dead in front of him, where the brother delighted in his younger sibling's horror as he promptly did. Where does one put these experiences without guidance? His dad, an abusive alcoholic, died shortly after we met, and on pressure from me a few months after, a DNA test proved his only child, aged ten by then, was not his. He'd not faced these things, nor knew how to – hence the reliance on drinking and often use of marijuana.

I had admired things in him, which I guess in hindsight were qualities I wanted for myself. Primarily, he never gave up, despite life's painful setbacks, and he always stood up for himself. At times he would have conflict with employers and speak up, which no doubt came across coarse and angry knowing his construction site colloquialisms; and if his employment ceased, he'd be immediately re-employed by his own efforts. He was a legend at anything to do

Chapter 17: The Giant

with construction, with impressive attention to detail with whatever he built or installed, and he was an incredible self-taught musician across instruments. The latter, however, he'd have to be off his rocker to escape his analytical mind and create spontaneously.

I don't care what anyone says promoting the contemporary acceptance of smoking weed. In my eyes, the person is never present with you. They're lost in their own mind and everyone else is plasma in the peripheral – and this was how I always felt. Such reliance on substances is how ignorance plays out in a world that tears us to shreds. I did have compassion for his experiences – I'd taught enough troubled teens to understand trauma, and the reliance on chemical remedies when people have no inner resources. But, in doing so, I rendered myself powerless and weak.

In the rare moments I had peace during this time, a gentle nudge kept floating to the foreground of my mind. It was about the quantum field and our influence on it. In the quiet observer's abstract fashion, I could see how I wanted conditions in my life to give me confidence and security, yet the truth was rather the opposite. If I changed perspective, fulfilling myself in these areas first, then the circumstances – and people – around me would reflect this. I was conflicted by this because I had difficulty accepting that people's mistreatment of me was a mirror of myself. To think there were different potentials for the same people was a real stretch at the time.

During the long, agonising weeks that followed, I was focused on the singular term 'Truth' in my disciplines – albeit interspersed between a crap-load of madness. I was like an alternating current, and my wires were burning from the speed of oscillation – literally. The problem was seeing truth through the lens of my hysterical personality, that became solely driven to show him the superficiality of online romance. I couldn't determine if getting through to him was an act of love or my desire to conquer and subdue. Despite the endless push and pull, I was compelled to reveal his shallowness – for his gain or mine – I was incapable of knowing in that state.

It occurred to me that he was reticent to accept his fading youth, and he felt safe expressing openness and intimacy via online texting. The tease and adoration of flirting with strangers allowed him to live in make believe and pretend the characters he and women projected were real, which was no doubt easier than the challenges of real-life relationships. I persuaded myself, quite effortlessly I might add, to venture into his world and tear away his delusion. If I couldn't rip it off, then at least I'd rip him a new one.

Let's just say I borrowed an old friend's social media images for my little enterprise. Since she was living on the other side of the world, hers weren't going to be noticed locally on a dating site, and I gave myself a day to do so. I set up a profile and waited. I didn't search him out and flirt – I knew from his phone I wouldn't have to. It took about an hour before he liked 'me'.

Before I elaborate on the course of events, let me pause and reflect on the value of our small and pathetic parts. To me, they are the markers that make us wonder if we can be anything greater – the propellants so to speak – that drive us forward. If we judge these aspects as shameful, we miss their purposefulness and spend our lives hiding them, which is why I've included them here. I never set out to write an altruistic book filled with spiritual fluff, as this would be an incomplete truth about uncovering what's in the soul.

I'd been present in Ram's audiences when he called out people's darkest secrets. He explained that calling them to the foreground reduced their fervour, and that he did so because he loved them. I remember being quietly relieved knowing some of the bigwigs on staff had done things I was also ashamed of. I learnt through this that God in us has never judged us, or none of us would be breathing today.

Whilst what transpired may in other circumstances be entertaining, I did not find it so. It was bloody torturous. He made fun of me and my UFO experiences – wrote me off entirely actually – all while I was encouraging him to do so.

Chapter 17: The Giant

The clincher, however, occurred at about 3p.m., after I had him convinced he was getting a leg over in the carpark at the end of the night. Silly bastard: I even got dick pics from him. I'd never seen one before and receiving them gave me the satisfying sense of having won. They don't realise their old fella looks more like it was taken from a cadaver, tawny and flaccid as it was – not one bit attractive, and I felt certain all women must have the same lip-pressing repulsion upon receipt.

Seamlessly, I had him arrive at a pub and order me a drink while I was 'stuck in traffic'. After I'd made him wait a decent amount of time, I sent him a screenshot of an email professing his love for me. Realising it was me all along, and receiving his vulgar two-word reply, I was glad I could end the charade. It was brutal to think he wasn't too dedicated to being celibate while fighting to have me back.

Trying to redeem himself once he was home, he joked that he'd shown the snap I'd sent of my butt to his flatmate. In reply, I sent one of his screenshots with the caption, "Show him this mess". It embarrassed him, and I copped about two hours of textual slurs thereafter. He'd made himself so vulnerable to a stranger, and the truth was confronting. The next morning, I left a voicemail that pretty much coined the situation as I saw it. I told him with an array of equally offensive adjectives and nouns that he was a balding, middle-aged man, chasing his pointy end around like a thirty-year-old – and needed to grow up.

Me too. I'd been seeking adulation and attention for having remodelled myself and was delusional in thinking some profound love would come of it. It seems we'd both been stuck in the nineties: he reliving his heyday, and me having never had one. It also revealed how much being the honourable adversary really positioned me as self-righteously superior, in that being the noble one meant the other party could feel perpetual guilt for their wrongs and give me the edge I could persecute them by.

Together we exposed our shadow selves, so I guess the scales were even. By then I had relieved myself of enough steam to see it was time to start my personal repair, and I could better distinguish between emotional deception from the personality and quiet prompts from the Observer. Essentially: beginning to decipher instinct from intuition. The personality, comprising our limiting attitudes and resulting propensities, is like a tragic song on repeat – and we feel it in the body as perpetual angst. The God in us, however, has a quiet, lingering presence that doesn't disturb. It's difficult to differentiate at first, but if we note the physical descriptions from the calm prompting, we begin to see things as they really are.

My eldest daughter returned to live on the Gold Coast during this and was over the moon to be near us again. I felt guilty that I was ruining her elation with my devastation, and made the difficult effort to meet at her beachside home with her sister. I could barely talk, but I did my best to hide it for their sake; as seeing the two, who'd had little interaction since my eldest had lived several years in Brisbane, walk and talk together, while our dogs swam in the sea, was quite special.

My youngest daughter had also given up the façade of the transgender thing, and doing so, she was no longer resistant to engaging with family. She'd bunged it on for two years, and I made every ingenuine effort to play along because of societal guilt – until one day I just lost it. She'd come downstairs putting on a man's voice, and being fed up, I yelled at her to cut the bullshit. I carried on about how she'd grown up insisting on wearing sparkly sandals, butterfly hairclips and mermaid costumes, and as her mum – I knew the bloody truth!

It could've gone either way, and I waited for the outcome. The next day, after hiding in her room all night, she said, "Look mum". She was wearing make-up and had put on a pretty bra. I think she

Chapter 17: The Giant

was secretly relieved someone gave her permission to stop the pretence. She'd been cutting herself so badly all over I'd even taken her to hospital once, and this too had ceased. She tries so hard to stay afloat, because her deep mind can take her on tangents beyond her age and experience.

By the time the three of us met up, I'd been on my eldest's case for over six months for the details of her giant UFO encounter. She never replied to my texts once! I know she's stepped aside from her experiences, even growing up in Ram's school with her own results, because her partner is an atheist. She doesn't want him to know anything about her life in this regard.

I understand where she's coming from, after all, she'd lost faith in men and considered herself lucky to have a gentle, kind-hearted one that she'd been patient enough to wait for. Her dad had abandoned her at six, her grandpa, who became her substitute dad, didn't contact her for five years after I'd married the muslim, and the latter was a dominating and frightening man she'd endured for too long.

Unlike her mum, she never had a proper boyfriend until she was twenty-two. She's a stand-out beauty, inheriting her dad's Nordic genes, and is six foot tall and lithe. At her coastal high school, students and teachers unfairly judged her by her looks, but she was instead gentle and unassuming, and focussed on her studies the whole time.

I'm sad that she doesn't have the inclination for spiritual things anymore, but that's her journey and not my duty to impose upon her. Perhaps in her eyes my misadventures have overshadowed the mysterious, despite both of us having experienced more than UFOs in the application of our disciplines.

Strolling along the sand, I took advantage of our time to quiz her on the details. She explained that I'd gone downstairs to focus with my Turkish friend, and that I'd told her she had to go to bed for school. She included that she was disappointed, and sitting on her bed, which was pressed up against the large window, she did her grid discipline alone.

Very quickly into it, she saw something emerge from the roof above her that was wider than the window. It was so broad, she described, that she couldn't definitively say whether it was round or linear in shape, but that she felt it was circular. The width was undetectable because she couldn't see the sides, and it was so large that it felt as if its emergence above her would never end. It was silver, with no parts or seams, and no vents or such to disrupt the smooth flat surface. Rows of intense white lights repeated from the perimeter in, such that as the centre of the craft passed over her, she could see they made concentrically smaller circles, demonstrating that it was in fact round.

I recalled to her how I'd gone to her room that night to tell her about the silver boomerang, that my friend had astoundingly not seen, and reminded her that she'd said it was so big she was frightened. I pressed her further to elaborate how she felt as this occurred. I was surprised to hear her say that as it slowly passed, she wished it to stop for her, and that she was asking them to take her up. Interesting, considering she'd said it was so large she got scared, but perhaps this was her youthful choice of words at the time.

What was puzzling to me about this, was that I was sitting downstairs only metres away from her window with my stationary space craft, yet I had not seen this gargantuan one above! The size of the building we occupied was about fifty metres long, with only two floors, so if it was too wide for my daughter to see the sides then this monster had to have been close to a hundred metres in diameter. And if it was just above our roof, then it was roughly ten metres above my head; and I can honestly say, if it'd been uncloaked, it would've occupied a considerable space above me for some time with its slow glide above us! As I've said earlier, they know exactly who is meant to see, and since my friend didn't see what was directly in front of her, it seems I too was not ready to have such an encounter. Incredible mastery over physics and the human mind.

Chapter 17: The Giant

I wish I could say what followed in ensuing months was simple, but when you've had a lifetime of perceived rejection and hurt from the ones closest to you, the insecurity stored in the brain and biology is a battle of gigantic proportions. Mastering this, when our amygdala is designed to act on long term memory to keep us vigilant, to moving into knowing one is an indestructible God, is no easy feat. I recalled Dr Greer once said that right before atoms reform after breaking down they go into a kind of frenzy. This must've been where I was in my life, and it felt like living in a beehive.

During those months, or should I say enduring those months, I had some humbling realisations. Firstly, I remembered Ram saying that energy returns the way it went out; and since I'd started to resource my own worth in the preceding year, the energy distributed out from my vanity and superficiality had to be called back in kind. This was my rubber band snapping back – and naturally – it burned. I could also see the gut-heaving crying was nothing to do with betrayal and was instead a response to knowing I'd exhausted the gamut of my human resources. I was laid bare at my own alter – and by my own hands.

Passing through this reminded me of the large labyrinth at Ram's school that mimics the brain. It's an intense discipline that we do blindfold, and the rooms, caverns and tunnels take us symbolically from social consciousness to the deeper levels of the divine, according to our ability to remain focused. When we're emotionally affected, we'll be caught up in gruelling confines with near hysterical people, yet when we remain focused, remarkably we'll be guided into the quiet recesses. I loved it; and in my few occasions, at times I was able to channel myself effortlessly to some areas that resembled the mysterious layers of our brains.

Present in my mind today, and during my hellfire, is the recurring thread delivered by Ram of remaining focused in the midst of chaos. I was once in Yelm where he'd given the entire evening of teachings in poetry. Enchanting. The topic was the perpetuating patience of trees, remaining firm and resilient during storms and harsh climate, bearing the heavy load of snow, and dreaming of its new abundant growth in the warmer months. I am using this concept when my body is buzzing with discomfort, and my smaller mind is pulling me in directions I'm no longer interested in. The simpleness of symbols in our mind: they contain so much information yet are not heavy with emotion. Imagery is such a sublime language.

I also found myself reflecting often on Shakespeare's allusion that all the world is a stage, and we are merely actors. This has a kind of contractual connotation attached to the players we have enter and exit our lives. If we design our lives beforehand, for the purpose of finding our way back to divinity, then there can be no blame upon anyone – or regret. Everyone has played their characters superbly, and me for theirs. If I had decided before I was born that I wanted to know love, then this script has been perfect. If I commit myself hereafter to knowing self-love, then insecurity must eventually dissolve away.

CHAPTER EIGHTEEN

The Interaction

I have now embarked on a very intense, personal campaign to change my brain and chemistry, to mirror the intangible part of me. At times it's more like pushing shit uphill, as my past still rolls out to the present and the chemicals of emotional addiction linger in my body. The lethargy one experiences when changing is incredible, but I can subtly view the resistance as just my cells calling, separate from myself as the Observer. Despite the difficulty, something propels me to keep going: I must be starting to *know* I am God.

Wondering where to start, it occurred to me I had to rewrite my long-term memory. If the amygdala is triggered by situations stored from my past, alerting me of imaginary threats, then it is logical that I create new memories of my experiences. The past no longer exists, just as the future is yet to be experienced, and if the brain does not distinguish truth from imagination, then I can decide what is true. Therefore, which version of truth do I want to subscribe too? The victim of my past or a different experience of it? I can have all my events as they were, but I can shift my subjective perception of them.

This is where the earlier concept of changing oneself to alter the quantum field of experience became quietly illuminated for me. I could choose to overlay my history with having always been secure, empowered, decisive, and self-loving in all my experiences. I would have the wisdom from them, but without the attachments of threat that my original long-term memory presently has.

This is in the realm of my acceptance, based on several of my experiences of the supernatural, but I'll draw on two described in this book. Consider when I had seen the two-foot owl, which obviously wasn't: who was really responsible for that perception? I had thought the overlay was the extra-terrestrial's doing to prevent fear, but I'm now postulating that I projected that according to my own free-will. Similarly, whose truth was reality, when myself, my daughter, and my friend, each saw vastly different events simultaneously on the night of the silver boomerang and the giant? It must be that each of our quantum realities are entirely constructed by our subjective truth and expectation.

Bearing in mind too, if I occupy my Observer in rewriting my reality, this zero-point in time and space is like a beacon shining in all directions. My past, present, and future, are all ascribed with the new imprint – that's the beauty of the term 'always'. Given that our acceptance motivates us, I am excited by the concept of having creative control over my life, as opposed to needing the original program. To do this then, I needed to persistently work at building new neural wiring. And from this revelation, I had a brief, other-worldly experience shortly after.

I was downstairs in the dark doing the focused walk around the kitchen and lounge when I was interrupted by a particular idea and how to include it in this book. It came to me that the building of new neural pathways was the means of explaining the *purpose* and *effect* of the disciplines. Immediately in front of me, an explosion of linear white streams burst out of something invisible in the air. The spectacle was silent, and the thick filaments of light appeared rapidly in succession – faster than I can blink. They were longer at the top and bottom, with graduations in length as they splayed out from a blackened centre. Like the red lights, it had a technological

Chapter 18: The Interaction

appearance rather than ethereal, but I could not see what was emanating them as the lights did not illuminate any object, nor the air around it. It lasted only about five or six seconds, but long enough for me to examine every detail as I've learnt to do.

I laughed softly to myself, knowing I was still being monitored. It was comforting to know I had overseers on this difficult path. "Yes, ok", I said smiling, "I'll make sure that goes in".

In quiet reflection over the months, I began asking my Observer what attitudes and limiting traits I had that I couldn't see, and why I had perpetual burning in my nerves all night. The gentle bleeding out of information revealed I was conditioned to live with relentless resentment, from years of having to tolerate my mum growing up, and I was thus accustomed to having close relationships that were indifferent, as a result. I had similarly subsumed my dad's qualities of selflessly putting up with it for the chemical outpouring it afforded – enormous self-pity. He too was the intellectual type and was able to obscure a person's faults to justify his loyalty, despite an absence of love or appreciation towards him.

It must be reiterated, however, that it's not only that these qualities were adopted through nurture, but that they were equal to my energetic signature upon conception. The DNA pairing was exactly my frequency to enter, as we only get precisely what we are. And since our cells are programmed according to the qualities we inhabit, my DNA – in every single cell – screamed out for situations that elicited the chemical signatures to feed it accordingly. In simple terms, I engaged in thoughts and situations that fed the cells their drug of choice.

This begs the question then: why are we different from our siblings if we were frequency specific to the combination of our parents? I would suggest this is because our parents aren't singular in their qualities, just as we are also multi-faceted in ours. We have different friends for varying parts of ourselves who may never meet, and each would have a different summation of who we are according to their own experiences with us.

My new understanding of unconscious paradigms governing our lives finally explained why I had horrendous anxiety *after* my marriage dissolved and following the most recent one. For years after removing my husband, I could not for the life of me determine why I'd have such debilitating panic if the horrible circumstances had been eradicated and life made easier. It was, quite illuminatingly, because my addictions were not being met. Strange, I know, but our paradigms in the emotional body are so concrete, and it is their loss that threatens them.

In my expose of self, I also received startling insight into my decade's long confusion distinguishing right from wrong in relationships. My justifying why I stayed so long in strenuous situations had first been attributed to my inability to decipher what love should look like, based on my mashed-up experiences in childhood. I used to torment myself wondering if I was being judgemental, having unfair expectations, or that I wasn't being allowing – me being my dad, essentially. Then I had one of those sudden flashes containing the complete gnosis: there was never confusion, only denial. God. That was big. I was always arguing to defend my addiction to emotions, and nothing less.

From all this clarity blame naturally – and very reluctantly I might add – began to dissipate. Towards my parents, to my work, and to the men I kept prisoner for too many years. I would be a fool to say this was done and dusted, as I know things like this take persistent diligence in eliminating them. For me, this process was the slow turning of my sword of endurance to its other face.

The first step in this unravelling required what I call the *Rumpelstiltskin*, named after the forgettable fairytale, that is a spiritual tool in plain sight. I can't recall where I heard about this hidden gem, or even if I arrived at it myself from teaching English, but

Chapter 18: The Interaction

that is irrelevant. When you examine the tale, you'll see there is a tormented young mother pacing her room trying to figure out the intruding imp's name or surrender her first child to him if she doesn't. When she is finally able to name her necromancer, the troublesome creature is never seen again. This is reminiscent of our own selves kept awake in long restless nights, endeavouring to figure out the causes of our suffering with little resolve. It is this concept I apply in two ways; and although Ram has a more specific method to this, I've adapted it with progressive success and will briefly elaborate on what I do.

Its use began with one of those flashes that came, revealing that I'd spent years trying *not* to feel all the horrible emotions I was experiencing, serving only to power up those beasts that screamed to be heard. My first step in dissolving them was to acknowledge and allow the full rush of chemicals as they occurred in any moment. I immediately labelled them with a single word, and held my attention solely on the physical responses for several minutes. Unjudging, and without revisiting the scenarios they were attached to, I let anxiety, anger, regret, resentment, humiliation, denial, and self-pity have their spotlight for a brief period until they exhausted their charge. This is not to say that was the end of them after once or twice – no way – I spent tedious months identifying and focusing my attention on them.

Having my key terms known, I also applied – and still do – these singular words in my disciplines for the Observer to unleash the hold they have over me. I know that the overseer in the back of my head has no ideology of good or bad about these emotions, and does not need me to sit during focus and explain what I want done with them – it is *known*. And of note: I'm not recreating them. By looking impartially at them they are only an uncharged concept. I was similarly conscious that the vacuum created needed to be filled with new paradigms, and I was vigilant to balance my disciplines with building new concepts and a freer future.

From these processes, I know I am gradually changing my energy field's frequency and rewriting my DNA; and one day, my propensities will be unlocked from addiction and morphed into wisdom.

The premise of being God is that we create reality using our consciousness. In this realm, and occupying a physical body, our brains engage the quantum field to later experience concepts in matter. To do this means utilising neuronal connections. When used regularly, they become hard-wired and our life correspondingly reflects this, so to have a more expanded reality – or even simply change – we must use different circuitry. This is how disciplines, so called for obvious reasons, essentially do this.

Upon waking, or going to sleep, the brain is very receptive by the more powerful frequencies it has been emitting immediately preceding and during sleep. It's the perfect time to engage with ourselves as God. Not stopping there though, any time of day we apply ourselves is slowly building new pathways which will affect our future. I am now spending a larger portion of my day, and into the hours of the night, doing my array of disciplines. Even when I'm casually about my activities, and I find myself lost in rampant thinking, I intercede and return to my set of commands, or picture singular words or symbols for rewiring.

This raises a good question: who is commanding, and what are we making commands to? Try this little exercise to know for yourself. This came to me by my own inspiration, and I refer to it for redirection when I find myself doing disciplines unfocused. Imagine yourself *as* your body, then think of the intangible, spiritual part of you for a moment. You can distinctly see yourself in two parts, but the intangible part is the 'other' contained in you. Next: position your mind now as that invisible part and imagine this *in* the body looking out. Take a few moments to picture it. Notice you swapped perspectives? When we move awareness to the intangible aspect, we

Chapter 18: The Interaction

become the Observer: our Soul, who Socrates termed the Oracle. So, what part of us, then, transforms the commands into matter? The emanating force: the Spirit.

When we make commands to our spirit, we are better served commanding it from the perspective of the Observer as opposed to our body-associated consciousness that is tainted with emotional bias. For decades, and occasionally when I forget, I did my disciplines from the latter perspective – talking *to* God, not *as* it. I am now making it a habit to first place myself as the Observer before focus until it sinks in. For me, this means I'm taking the position of objectivity rather than the past-anchored personality.

It must be noted from my experience that there is no emotional response when engaged in the disciplines as quantifiers for it working. Physical sensations? Yes – sometimes – but I won't put ideas in people's heads to artificially evoke them, I'll leave that for one's own experience to note. Expecting a good emotion during disciplines is a waste of mind, because we've never experienced what we're focussed on – they're unknowns – so we would be fantasising based on feelings we've already experienced, and associated therefore, with the past. They must be clean.

I'm finally figuring out that matters of the intangible are whisper soft in experience, hence why we miss them most of the time. Moments of elemental love, contentment, and sparks of knowingness don't elicit the emotional surges we feel. The intensity of rage, malice, betrayal, and the like, are more seductive than heroin, and as the song says, cause us to bleed to know we're alive – while they quietly ravage the body.

If we wish to heal, or even if we do this to initiate contact with ETs, if that's a goal, I recommend focussing on ourselves first. By doing this we pull all our energy drained out toward people and situations back to self. A challenging concept – I know. Then, practice distinguishing between emotions and quiet knowingness to determine what new concepts need to be wired.

This is where disciplines can be applied to provide conscientious direction. I've been doing disciplines long enough to troubleshoot and differentiate the state of mind needed to make progress, which has been painstakingly slow given my propensities for emotional BS. I know for myself that mindless chatter takes about 15 to 20 minutes to dull down, which is why I prefer undisturbed nights, but I expect this latency period to be reduced with practice. I have gauged progress, however, by my incrementally less reactive responses to incidences, and the emotional recovery period is also shorter.

The challenge is also to have the same gusto in doing them when times are good. Nothing like adversity to put a cracker up our ass, but the tokenistic quality of them when we have good days is where our determination drops off. Just when I think I've mastered something and stop giving it my focus, an incident pops up and I experience upheaval again, showing it wasn't properly integrated. To hardwire a new and better future requires continued action and attention.

At Ram's school, the first discipline I learnt was doing the List® upon waking and going to sleep. Strangely, I never liked doing this, because I have a natural rebellion when it's a must-do at specific times. I'd always gladly do the other ones because they could be at my leisure, so to speak, but I think now in understanding how it works I've matured with it. I've also made my list, which is a set of self-designed instructions, into audios of my voice to sometimes play when I'm out with the dog, cleaning or driving. Even when I do laps at the pool, I'm holding key words or symbols, or doing the list. I want to flood my mind as often as possible, a lot like the constant persuasion of advertising – I am making my own.

When I'm not in good mental shape, I'll start with the walking one I mentioned earlier, as the movement tends to focus my mind if I'm stuck in incessant thinking. It involves speaking slowly out loud with pauses between sentences for neurons to form the abstract imagery. Another active one I do when I'm caught up in fear or other emotions is Ramtha's explosive breathing technique. This one is worth elaborating on.

Not to be confused with deep breathing, this is killer number one to removing chaos in our mind, as well as for manifesting. I've had an immediate healing during one of these, as well as other miracles, when done correctly and consistently. We really need to have proper induction on this technique, as it employs the brain, will, frequencies of energy, and focused imagery, on top of the very particular way the breathing is done. Called Consciousness and Energy®, or C&E®, for all the reasons listed above, this is my go-to in my walk-in-robe, and it's best done with loud energetic music.

If I'm feeling deflated and the body is heavy with resistance, I'll do Twilight®. A seemingly passive and easy discipline compared to others; yet when done correctly, I am lightened and at greater ease afterwards. It is the engaging of dreamy stillness right before sleep, only the goal is to stay awake. If we nod off and are able to rouse ourselves, we promptly return to our image of focus. Ram explains that we must lie flat and straight, because the natural foetal position we ordinarily do is associated with sleep, and not focus. That said, I do employ my focus during regular sleeping positions if I awaken in the night – it's all reiterating my intent to the Spirit.

If I am steadier in my mind and body, I'll do a seated discipline I have modified for myself. Often, I focus on holding the image of the cobalt blue Shiva as my own body, which Ram calls the Blue Body®. This discipline is primarily designed for physical healing, and usually involves darkened eyes with dancing, but I am using it largely in still focus. Its associated frequency has expansive consciousness that is closer to the Source than my fractured personality, and I combine it with the grid when done this way.

You may benefit from reading Roald Dahl's *The Wonderful Story of Henry Sugar*. Champion little discipline hidden in that true account, using the candle I referred to earlier. Of note: I don't place the image in the candle that the story recommends, but instead place ones that better hold my attention for sustained periods – usually whatever it is I am passionate about in that moment. During this, I get an innate sense of connection with the soul, but this is perhaps because it is said the inner darkened portion of the flame represents the Soul, and the brighter exterior that of the Spirit, and I accept it.

Bear in mind that it's best to have no expectations attached to the outcome of the disciplines. The purpose of them is to open our brain, and like the alchemist turning gold from other materials – they did not do them in one sitting. Ram said they take years because the alchemist cannot take their mind and eyes away from the concoction too long, essentially holding the singular image into fruition. Will this process take years or decades? Probably. I don't care. What else is there? I have passed through enough drama to know that physical reality is just a construct of static dreams – and my mind is its Master curator. And, gratefully, I am finally made patient by my agonising misdeeds and misdirection. Thank God!

Does this mean we give up living and socialising? Definitely not. I now understand the value of human connection, contributing to life, and enjoying it too, but I am guarded in my use of time and interactions. I've considerably distanced myself from friends, except a select few I can speak meaningfully with, because my time for focus is too valuable, and I also don't want to reaffirm my old dilemmas and conditions in conversation. I know everyone has their responsibilities, such as work, maintaining a home and family, but to what end is keeping up appearances or over-working if it steals us from finding peace and discovering our incredible mind and abilities?

Overall, we must fulfill our needed experiences along the way, but I recommend being wiser than me by distinguishing fact from fiction, as I've already described. If I'd have taken more time to connect with my Observer, to know the lure of fantasy and emotional entanglement, I could've had inklings of future outcomes to make happier choices. Ram did say once that slow growing trees

Chapter 18: The Interaction

have the strongest wood, so I have no choice but to see my painful follies as purposeful. Interestingly, we have trees in Australia that require being burnt in a bushfire to germinate seeds – what an ironic metaphor for perpetual growth!

Contemplating the white intensity that appeared after years of nothing, I was again pondering the timeliness and purpose of the visitor's appearance. It would be more accurate to use the term timelessness, as clearly the occupants are operating outside of its confines, and I again wondered how much I had to do with it. If I was evolved enough somewhere in my future – be it a hundred years, a thousand, or a million – could I have been an occupant to come back and strengthen my resolve? This would account for the craft's radiant appearance exactly during my revelation regarding the indomitable spirit. I will contemplate this and await the knowingness.

Startlingly, I had another encounter, quite unlike my others. I'd finally started doing my grid outside again, and on my third go a star turned on in my gaze. Sitting about forty-five degrees up, it had consistent blinking on and off, and I noted its difference to the smaller star to its right, that twinkled ordinarily. It was stationary for some minutes, as I compared the two, concluding they were not the same. It wasn't a drone, as my fella had had a few, and one costing several thousand dollars with exceptional manoeuvrability, so I knew their capabilities. Drones have limits to their elevation, as well as their battery life, and being manually operated, don't remain exactly in one fixed position for too long. Their lighting is different at night, too. This had a complete illumination when blinking, unlike a drone that has smaller flashing lights.

Pondering these possibilities, a plane then passed into view from my right at about the same height, with its distinct alternating flash of red and white lights, and low engine hum. I knew then that this was a UFO. Just as my eyes shifted back from the plane, it dropped vertically from its high position to directly in front of my gaze, just above the tree line. Motionless, it continued to blink in its consistent fashion.

I smiled, noting it had descended the moment I decided it was something else. The flight downward had the weightlessness of a spider in freefall, but with more intentional momentum. In this spot, it occasionally ceased flashing, and became invisible for moments at a time in my mind. Each time it disappeared; I asked them to come back for me – if they loved the God in me – which they promptly did. I wondered if they were genuinely connecting with me, given their timely responsiveness, or if I was reading too much into it.

I also requested they take me up. 'I'm ready guys', I said several times. Then the fear began jetting through me. The craft remained in this fixed spot while I addressed this, and I insisted to them, 'I would be initially scared, but promise to have the wherewithal to deal with it'. Just as I said this, the star then glided left a fair distance, horizontal and smooth, where it stayed for a few more minutes, still blinking and perfectly stationary. After another few minutes, it then effortlessly moved back to its position of initial descent and remained still for a while longer.

During it all, I held the image of a blue star inside its craft, not knowing what that interior really consisted of, to indicate my connection with them non-locally. At one point I considered trying to film it, because it was an extended encounter, but I deduced it wouldn't take to my old smartphone camera. This event was tens of kilometres away in my estimation, and I'd filmed a full moon on the horizon before, as well as Venus, and the images are generally disappointing. From these deductions, I decided the video wouldn't prove anything.

Just as I concluded this, it suddenly propelled towards me. Taking only a few seconds to jet in total silence to a few streets away, I noted its increasing brightness and the density of light in every pulse. 'Holy shit! Is this it? Are they actually coming for me?!', I thought with halted breath. Then, as if responding to my fear, it simply disappeared. Not disappointed, and laughing to myself, I marvelled that it had reacted to my mind on point for every query, across the ten or twelve minutes.

I couldn't say it had the dazzling display of some of the others, but this one demonstrated connection. Perhaps there were other people outside wondering the same thing, and they too had similar questioning it responded to. We may all have had a collective experience – and I won't assume it was just my own on this occasion. Content knowing it appeared in my focus, as many have before, I had the additional layer of this time engaging in responsive interaction. This may be the first steps to eventually having awake, face-to-face meetings.

No doubt I have a lot of work to do in restoring stillness to my brain, and having the qualities worthy of such experiences, but I say, "Yeah baby!!"

The biggest secret held from all humanity is not that infinite life exists in the universe, with its unlimited varieties of life-forms and civilisations, but that every single one of us ordinary people are living Gods. A tragedy for this to be covered up for so long, and this alone makes it a prison planet. Once this begins to bleed out – and it is – watch things change here on Earth and expect the great ones to come.

And to the many unanswered 'whys' of having incredible craft with me in quiet observation: I'm going to say, "All of the above".

There is nothing held back from us in our design, as our brain contains everything needed as the interface to being God. To become our divine selves, we must first be the Sourcerer. And, if Will can be sustained amidst the chaos this process unfolds, we can eventually *become* The Source. It just depends on how much we want it.

About the Author

The author, simply called Miss by thousands of high school students, has a bachelor's degree in education but credits her most genuine learning from Ramtha's School of Enlightenment and the school of hard knocks.

www.ingramcontent.com/pod-product-compliance
Lightning Source LLC
Chambersburg PA
CBHW062037290426
44109CB00026B/2645